Rigatoni

ardelle

Maltagliati

THE PASTA
MACHINE
COOKBOOK

THE PASTA
MACHINE
COOKBOOK

GINA STEER

A QUINTET BOOK

Published by the Apple Press
6 Blundell Street
London N7 9BH

ISBN 1-85076-782-3

This book was designed and produced by
Quintet Publishing Limited
6 Blundell Street
London N7 9BH

Creative Director: Richard Dewing
Art Director: Clare Reynolds
Designer: Isobel Gillan
Project Editor: Clare Hubbard
Editor: Barbara Croxford
Photographer: Philip Wilkins, except pages 20, 22, 23
and main jacket image by David Armstrong

Typeset in Great Britain by
Central Southern Typesetters, Eastbourne
Manufactured in Singapore by
Pica Colour Separation Overseas Pte. Ltd.
Printed in Singapore by
Star Standard Industries (Pte.) Ltd.

Picture Credits
Life File: pages 7, 19, 28, 40, 59, 76, 93;
Peter Wilson: pages 105, 121.

Acknowledgements
The publisher would like to thank
O.M.C. MARCATO s.r.l. for supplying the Atlas Regina
Extruder machine featured on pages 8 and 25.

CONTENTS

INTRODUCTION

There are few greater pleasures in life to me than eating. I am sure most people would agree with this and perhaps one of the greatest and most versatile of all foods has to be pasta. From being the staple diet of all Italians, pasta has quickly become popular everywhere, evolving over the years from just simple noodles or ribbons to the many different shapes, colours and flavours which we all now enjoy—offering the most wonderful taste sensation to all discerning palates.

There are two main types of pasta—flour and water pasta and egg pasta. Flour and water pasta is made from durum wheat flour (a high gluten flour, called semolina in Italy), and these pastas include the ever faithful spaghetti, tubes, such as rigatoni and many other shapes which complement strong, spicy, zesty sauces.

Then there is egg pasta, which is made from flour and eggs. The flour used here is a soft wheat flour which, outside Italy, is equivalent to a plain flour. However, there are some who say that durum wheat flour must be used for both kinds of pasta and, in some areas of Italy, olive oil and salt are added. Egg pastas absorb sauces far more readily than the flour and water pastas, and are well suited to egg, butter and cream sauces. Egg pasta is very delicate with a thin texture. It

is, therefore, important when making this pasta to keep the pasta warm during the making and handling. The best way to store it is to let it dry completely and then keep at room temperature in jars.

Although there are many commercially made pastas available, many cooks enjoy the challenge of making their own pasta, as the flavour and texture of home-made pasta is far superior to store bought. Owning your own pasta-making machine takes much of the hard work and effort out of the job and helps to make home-made pasta far more achievable. They are simple to use and once the basic techniques have been mastered, you will be able to make the most delicious pasta meals with great expertise and very little effort.

As well as a pasta-making machine, there are a few other basic pieces of equipment and tools that you will need when making home-made pasta (see page 9). They are all easily obtainable from kitchen shops or large department stores. You will most probably find that you already possess most of them in your kitchen.

There are a few simple techniques that are vital for a successful result and, providing you follow these techniques when you first embark on making your own pasta, I guarantee that you will not fail in serving delicious pasta every time.

CHAPTER ONE

PASTA KNOW-HOW

BEFORE YOU BEGIN MAKING YOUR PASTA MAKE SURE YOU KNOW HOW TO USE YOUR MACHINE CORRECTLY AND THAT YOU HAVE ANY OTHER NECESSARY EQUIPMENT AT HAND. THIS CHAPTER WILL EQUIP YOU WITH THE BASIC KNOWLEDGE TO GET YOU STARTED, INCLUDING A GUIDE TO THE ESSENTIAL INGREDIENTS THAT YOU NEED TO MAKE DELICIOUS PASTA DISHES.

PASTA MACHINES

When using your pasta machine for the first time, don't expect a perfect result; like everything, practise makes perfect, but the results amply justify the effort.

There are many different pasta machines available on the market. Some simply roll out the pasta dough and cut it into varying ribbon widths; there are attachments available for these machines for making other pastas such as ravioli and cannelloni. Other machines actually mix the pasta dough and have many attachments for making an assortment of shapes as well as ribbons and ravioli. Some are electrically operated, some are hand operated. In all cases it is vital that the manufacturer's instructions are thoroughly read before using your machine for the first time as the machines vary slightly. In this book we have tried to show you the main types of machine that are available in kitchen shops and department stores and we have given you the essential information so that no matter what type of machine you have, the pasta you produce will be perfect.

USING YOUR HAND-OPERATED MACHINE

Before using your machine for the first time, wipe down thoroughly with a clean cloth to remove any excess oil. After you have finished using your machine, wipe down with a clean, soft, dry cloth or, if preferred, brush with a soft brush. With regard to the rolling and cutting machine, **never, never** wash in detergent or water as the intricate parts will not work properly. If excess pasta has dried on the machine, just knock lightly and the pasta will fall off. **Take care** with the cutter section as this is a separate section of the machine and should be removed for cleaning and to prevent it falling off accidentally.

Never insert knives or sharp points in between the rollers. If desired, the ends of the cutting rollers can occasionally be smeared with a little oil if they are sticking slightly.

Below A hand-operated extruder machine cuts different pasta shapes depending upon which cutter you attach.

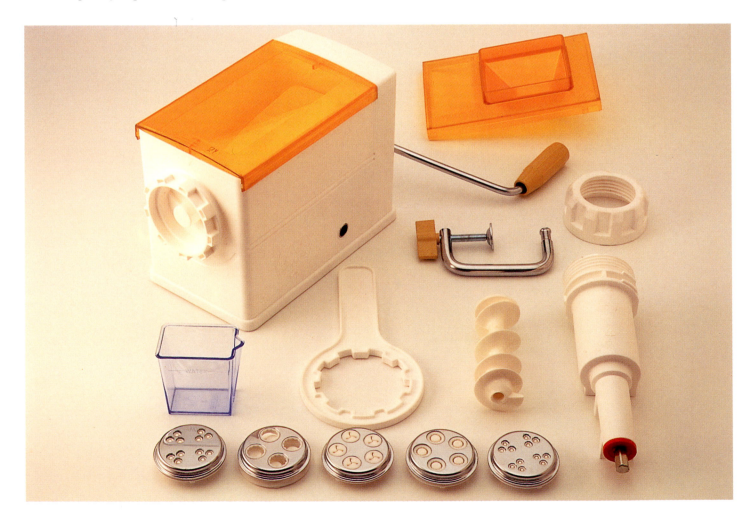

ELECTRICALLY OPERATED MACHINES

When using your electrically operated machine for the first time, **read the instructions** before you do anything else. Unpack the machine and check that it is complete. The machine should not be used by children and remember **never** leave the machine plugged in when not in use or when cleaning or carrying out any maintenance. If in doubt, contact your nearest stockist or an authorised dealer.

Ensure that the plug on the machine is correctly fitted—that the earthing of the socket is correct and the power supply corresponds to the data on the machine.

Never try to remove the extruder when in use—a safety device is fitted to ensure that the machine will not work when the lid is removed, so it is important to ensure that the machine is assembled correctly before switching on.

Thoroughly clean the machine after use; wash all parts that come into contact with food.

Below An electrically operated pasta machine.

Make sure the machine has a thermostat fitted which will automatically switch off the machine if it overheats. Normally, after 15–20 minutes it will start up again. If the machine has been in operation for more than 25 minutes, this may result in the machine switching itself off.

When using any of the extruders, immerse in hot water, then dry thoroughly and fit to the machine. To clean the extruders after use, immerse in hot soapy water, leave to soak for a few minutes, then with a hard bristle brush knock out any food residue. Dry thoroughly.

When mixing in the machine, it is important to use the correct quantity of flour and liquid (**refer to recipe given in manufacturer's instructions**). The slide must always remain in the machine and the mixture should be neither too wet nor too dry. When beginning to use the machine, the first batch extruded can be irregular in shape until the machine has warmed up.

EQUIPMENT

Dough Scraper—this is made from plastic or metal and is ideal for scraping the sticky dough off the work surface before kneading, prior to rolling.
Fork—this is just an ordinary fork which is used to mix the flour and eggs together to make the pasta dough.
Grooved Wooden Butter Shaper—this is used to give the ridged effect on pasta shapes; a wooden pencil or piece of dowel is also used to make tubes.
Pastry Cutter—used for cutting out filled ravioli, if you do not have the ravioli cutter for your machine. Also used for cutting lasagne sheets.
Biscuit Cutters—plain or fluted, for cutting out rolled pasta when making tortelloni, etc.
Kitchen Knife—used for cutting, chopping, etc.
Grater—used for grating cheese.
Large Saucepan—you will need a very large saucepan as pasta needs to be cooked in plenty of boiling water.
Colander—ideal for straining the cooked pasta. If preferred, you can use a draining spoon for removing stuffed pasta.
Teatowels—you will need some clean teatowels so that the rolled pasta shapes or filled pastas can be left to dry before cooking.
Clingfilm—this is required to wrap the prepared pasta dough to prevent it from drying out before filling.
Food Processor—this can be used if liked to make the dough, although you will still need to knead the dough.

Pasta Catalogue

There are many different pasta shapes, colours and flavours available and one would need a book by itself to list every single one that is made, both in and out of Italy; also, many pastas have different names depending on which region of Italy you are in. Listed below are the most commonly known and used pastas including shaped pastas that are easy to make in your pasta machine or by hand once you have used your machine to roll out the dough.

Long and Ribbon Pasta

The most well known are perhaps spaghetti, fettuccine and tagliatelle. Most sauces served with long pastas contain small pieces of food rather than large chunks. This is so that the sauce ingredients cling to the pasta when it is twirled on a fork. But, of course, this is only a general rule and rules are made to be broken.

Long Pasta

Angel Hair *(Capelli D'Angelo)* **(1)**—an extremely fine, long pasta, very light and delicate in appearance. Ideal if served with a soup and makes an ideal pasta to serve as a dessert.

Spaghetti (2) (can also be called vermicelli)—the best known of all pastas, commercially available in a wide range of colours.

Spaghettini (3)—the "ini" at the end of pastas means small, so this pasta is smaller or thinner than spaghetti.

Ribbons

Fettuccine (4)—narrower than tagliatelle: 5 mm/$\frac{1}{5}$ inch wide. Perfect for both appetizers and main courses.

Pappardelle (5)—a wide pasta about 2 cm/$\frac{3}{4}$ inch wide.

Tagliatelle (6)—about 8 mm/$\frac{1}{3}$ inch wide. Comes from the Italian word *tagliare*: "to cut." Perhaps one of the most well known of the ribbon pastas. Ideal with rich, meaty sauces.

Taglioni (7)—a very narrow pasta about 2 mm/$\frac{1}{16}$ inch wide.

Pasta Shapes

There is an immense variety of special shaped pastas, all designed to catch the eye and appeal to our aesthetic senses. However, there is another role of the shaped pastas and that is to entrap more of the delicious sauces that are served with the pasta and thus increase our enjoyment while eating. Many of the shapes that are now available are commercially made. I have listed here the most popular shapes to try, using a pasta-making machine.

Brandelle (8)—ragged or torn small pieces of pasta dough.

Farfalle (9)—bow ties or butterflies.

Fusilli (10)—spiral shapes.

Garganelli (11)—an irregular shaped tube with jagged edge, traditionally made by hand.

Macaroni (12)—hollow tubes of pasta, larger than spaghetti.

Maltagliati —irregular shapes of pasta, cut out with a pastry cutter.

Orecchiette (13)—or "little ears."

Penne (14)—perhaps the most well known of tubes. Difficult to make by hand if you do not have a machine that actually makes and shapes penne. A good substitute for penne is garganelli, which is simpler and quick to make by hand. There is little difference in the look except that garganelli is more irregular.

Rigatoni (15)—Ridged tubes, like large ridged macaroni. Good for baked dishes.

1

2

3

4

5

6

4

8

9

7

10

11

12

13

14

15

FILLED PASTAS

Filled pastas incorporate cannelloni, lasagne, ravioli and tortelloni.

Cannelloni—sheets of lasagne that are stuffed and rolled, topped with a sauce and baked. Can be made using an attachment to your machine or by hand.

Lasagne—flat sheet of pasta about 13 cm/5 inches wide. Layered with meat, fish or vegetable sauce, often topped with cheese and baked.

Ravioli—small squares that are filled with a variety of different fillings, cooked and served tossed in a sauce (see page 24 to make). Can be made using a special attachment for your machine or by hand.

Tortelloni—similar to ravioli, often filled with Swiss chard or spinach and ricotta cheese. Can be similar to cappelletti, made from a round of pasta.

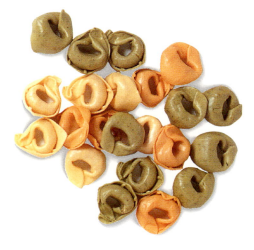

COLOURED AND FLAVOURED PASTAS

Coloured and flavoured pastas are more popular outside Italy. The only colours that can normally be found in Italy are red tomato pasta and green spinach pasta (*pasta verdi*). Coloured and flavoured pastas are easy to make and are an interesting and attractive alternative. (See pages 94 to 104 for recipes.)

Green—Spinach Pasta—also known as *verdi*. Made by adding finely chopped spinach. When rolled with the machine, the colour is very even.

Orange/Red—Tomato Pasta—made by adding tomato purée to the basic dough.

Yellow—Saffron Pasta—made by adding saffron strands.

Brown—Mushroom Pasta—made by adding finely chopped, soaked and dried mushrooms.

Black Pasta—made by adding squid ink.

Red—Beetroot Pasta—made by adding beetroot purée.

Brown—Chocolate Pasta—made by adding plain chocolate and sometimes unsweetened cocoa powder.

Herb Pasta—made by adding finely chopped fresh herbs.

Citrus Pasta—made by adding freshly grated lemon, lime or orange zest, or a mixture of all three.

PASTA LARDER

Some ingredients are so synonymous with pasta that I would not dream of being without them when cooking any pasta dish. Here I have listed the main ingredients that you can expect to find in this cookbook with simple explanations where necessary.

OIL AND VINEGAR

Extra Virgin Olive Oil The finest of all oils, ranging in colour from pale green to deep yellow, depending on the growing area and the olives used. It is made from a single cold pressing of the olives. Best used for dressings rather than sauces, as it would be wrong to heat extra virgin olive oil and risk losing its fine flavour and aroma.

Virgin Olive Oil A very fine oil but it does not quite have the same flavour and aroma as extra virgin olive oil. Better to be used for dressings or in sauces which do not have strong flavours and are only briefly heated so that the flavour of the oil comes through.

Pure Olive Oil A blend of refined olive oil and virgin olive oil and is the cheapest of the three. It is better suited for cooking as the flavour is less overpowering and does not conflict with the other ingredients.

Balsamic Vinegar The king of all vinegars that has been matured in oak caskets for up to 50 years. Use sparingly; its fine, full flavour goes a long way.

HAM

Pancetta Air-cured ham with the addition of spices, used a great deal in Italy. If pancetta is unavailable, lean smoked bacon can be used.

Parma Ham It is the fat from Parma ham that is so useful in sauces. Normally sold cut very thinly, an air-dried ham with a very distinctive flavour.

Prosciutto An air and salt-cured ham, aged for one year, that can be used in place of Parma ham.

CHEESE

ABOVE Cheese is an important ingredient in many pasta dishes.

Parmesan/Parmigiano Reggiano Only the cheese made in the region of Reggio Emilia is allowed to be called Parmigiano Reggiano. Made from cows' milk it has a grainy texture with a fine, distinctive flavour. Best bought in chunks and grated when required. It can be bought in larger pieces, cut into smaller portions, then wrapped well and stored in the refrigerator. This way it will keep for months.

Pecorino Romano A sheep milk cheese which has been aged for one year and is used mainly for grating. Has a sharper flavour than Parmesan.

Ricotta A soft cheese, similar to cottage cheese. Ideal as a binding agent and used in stuffings for filled pastas. It can be made from either cow, goat, or sheep milk. If watching your fat content, it is possible to buy a low-fat ricotta cheese, or you can substitute with cottage cheese.

Mozzarella Traditionally made from buffalo milk. Use grated or sliced on top of baked dishes, it can also be eaten raw. You can buy smoked and low-fat mozzarella.

Fontina A semisoft cheese, used for cooking where a good melting cheese is required.

Mascarpone Similar to a thickened double cream. Used traditionally in desserts such as Tiramisu or eaten as a table cheese with fresh fruit.

Dolcelatte A soft, mild, blue-veined cheese. The name means "sweet milk".

Gorgonzola A blue-greenish veined, soft, high-fat cheese from Lombardy. It has a sharp, pungent taste with a creamy texture. Often served at the end of a meal.

FISH

Tuna Used in several classic Italian dishes. As well as being canned in various oils, it is possible to buy tuna canned in spring water or brine if you are watching your calorie intake.

Anchovies The best anchovy fillets to buy are preserved in salt. Soak in water for 30 minutes and pat dry before use.

TOMATOES

Plum Tomatoes A good rich and full flavour, these should be used while still firm but ripe and red. The tomatoes grown in Italy are so full of flavour because they are ripened under the sun. As it is hard to reproduce this flavour, try using the alternatives listed below.

Sun-dried Tomatoes Available either in jars in oil or just dried in packages. Very concentrated, sweet flavour. Should be chopped and added to the sauce at the beginning of cooking.

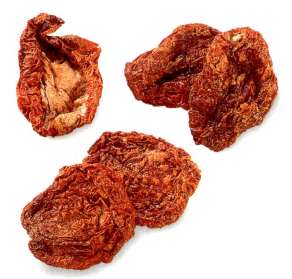

Canned Tomatoes Available in various forms. The best alternative to fresh plum tomatoes.

Tomato Purée Sold in tubes, jars or cans. An essential ingredient for many sauces for imparting an excellent tomato flavour.

Passata Creamed or pulped tomatoes, sold in jars or cans.

HERBS, SPICES, AND SEASONINGS

Garlic An essential ingredient for most cuisines. Always choose firm, plump heads. It is now possible to obtain smoked garlic; however, if you cannot find it, ordinary garlic can be used in its place and the flavour of the recipe will not be impaired.

Capers Choose capers that are preserved in salt for a better flavour. Soak in water for 30 minutes before use.

Olives Black olives are the ones generally used but the green olives from Southern Italy are excellent.

Basil As well as the familiar green-leafed basil, opal basil is available, which is a beautiful purple colour. Used extensively in salads as well as cooked dishes. Use at the end of cooking; tear or roughly chop before adding.

Flat Leaf or Continental Parsley Has a concentrated strong flavour, only worth using fresh.

Oregano A small leafed herb with a robust flavour.

Marjoram A spicy herb containing thymol in the leaves. Wild marjoram is also known as oregano and grows wild in Italy and Greece.

Rosemary Aromatic, spiky needle-type leaves with a very distinctive flavour. Grows wild in Italy and the Mediterranean.

Sage Aromatic velvety leaves in varying colours from green, to grey, to purple. Widely used in Italy.

Nutmeg An aromatic seed with a strong, distinctive flavour, originating in Indonesia. Best used freshly grated.

MUSHROOMS

Dried Mushrooms These are normally wild mushrooms and have a very strong, meaty flavour, so use sparingly. They need reconstituting in water before use. Use the soaking liquor in sauces, having strained it first. Normally sold sliced. Once opened, keep in an airtight container to preserve the flavour. Ceps are less expensive than morels. Morels have a very intense, bacon-like flavour and are dried whole. After soaking, they regain their original shape.

BELOW Mushrooms are an extremely versatile ingredient.

Wild Mushrooms Morels, chanterelles, ceps and girolles are the most widely sold wild mushrooms. They all have a very distinctive flavour.

Cultivated Mushrooms Shiitake and oyster mushrooms are now widely cultivated and provide a welcome addition to the familiar field or button mushrooms.

Truffles Perhaps one of the most expensive ingredients there is. Truffles cannot be cultivated and are "snuffed" out by pigs or dogs from under the ground. They are a fungi and available fresh from late autumn through to winter. The white truffle from Alba, Piedmont, is the king of all. Its flavour is so intense that you only need a very small amount. It is normally just grated fresh over the finished dish, **never** used for cooking. The black truffle from Umbria or Perigord (France) does not have such an intense flavour and is used for cooking. You can sometimes obtain truffles that have been preserved in oil. If unable to obtain either black or white truffles, use truffle oil, which gives a hint of the flavour. Available from good delicatessens and food stores.

Chillies Obtainable either fresh or dried. The heat is contained not only in the seeds but also in their membranes. Take care when handling; if the chilli juices get into your eyes, mouth, nose or an open wound, it smarts immensely. Wash hands thoroughly after use. Different chillies have different heat levels. As a general rule, the smaller the chilli, the higher the heat level. If in doubt, use a variety sparingly until you know its heat level. Dried chillies tend to be hot.

WINE NOTES

Wine must complement the food with which it is served. There are many wines to choose from, from all over the world. Whether you choose New World wines from California, Australia, New Zealand and South Africa, or you choose the more classic varieties from France, Italy and Spain, the same rules apply. The choice of wine depends not only on your personal palate but also on the food served and how it has been prepared. However, rules are continuously being broken and it is always a good idea to try a wide variety of the many wines that are so readily available.

Wines made from the same grape vary from region to region and from year to year. The amount of sun, the soil and the climate also play a critical part in the flavour and bouquet of the wine produced. Each producer combines different grapes and employs various methods in the production of their wines. There are so many excellent wines to choose from it would be a shame if you drank the same wines year after year.

With vinegary, citrus-based dishes or very strong spicy dishes, such as curries or chilli, it is pointless to serve a light, delicate wine or a robust wine; the acidity or spicy hot flavour of the dish will completely destroy the aroma and bouquet of the wine. It is better to serve chilled beer or lager or even a chilled mineral water in anticipation of the wines to come.

For pasta dishes that consist of fish, shellfish or vegetables, the type of wine to choose is the one that you would normally serve with fish or vegetables. Try well-chilled white wines with a good fresh tangy acidity and plenty of flavour such as Pouilly Fumé from France, or one of the New World wines such as Delegat's Hawkes Bay Sauvignon Blanc from New Zealand or Columbia Crest Sauvignon Blanc from Washington State.

Dishes that incorporate chicken are best served with either a full-flavoured white wine such as Cooks Chardonnay from New Zealand or a Chablis from France. You could also try a lighter red, such as Chianti Classico from Italy or Mountain View Pinot Noir from California.

Pastas with a meat sauce need strong robust wines, so a Tollana Cabernet-Shiraz from southern Australia or Merlot Collio from Italy would be ideal.

With any of the pastas that contain game, the general rule is that the stronger the flavour of the food, the more robust the wine required. A Burgundy such as Gevrey Chambertin from France would be ideal, as would Barolo from Italy or Jensen Vineyard Pinot Noir from California.

CHAPTER TWO

HOME-MADE PASTA

In this chapter you will find information and tips on making your own pasta, with some interesting and innovative new ideas for you to try when you have become proficient at pasta making. Easy-to-follow, step-by-step guides to using your pasta machine take the mystique out of the whole process.

BASIC PASTA DOUGH

The recipe below is ideal when making the dough by hand and using a pasta machine that rolls and cuts out basic shapes. However, some electrically operated machines and hand-operated extruders make the pasta as well. In this case, do check the manufacturer's instructions before using your machine for the first time. Plus, of course, there are some safety precautions when using an electrically operated machine that are critical (see page 9).

When making home-made pasta, ensure that the eggs are at room temperature and do not knead the dough on a very cold surface. Pasta dough needs to be kept warm while it is being made.

Makes 450 g/1 lb pasta dough

◆ 300 g/10 oz durum wheat flour (or Italian "OO" flour) or plain flour
◆ pinch of sea salt
◆ 3 medium eggs
◆ 1 tbsp virgin olive oil

1 Place the flour and salt in a mound on a clean work surface or in a large bowl. Make a well in the centre. Break the eggs one by one into the centre of the well and beat with a fork until the eggs are evenly mixed together. Add oil to the eggs.

2 Gradually incorporate the flour from inside the well into the egg until the egg is no longer runny. Take care not to break the wall of flour or the egg will escape. Using both hands, quickly bring the flour up over the egg mixture. Work until all the flour is mixed into the egg. Mix to form a stiff dough, adding a little water if necessary.

3 The dough should feel moist but not sticky. Wrap in clingfilm if not rolling immediately. Clean your hands and if necessary, the work surface. Hold the dough with one hand and fold it over with the fingers of the other hand. Knead the dough with the heel of your palm, rotating the dough a quarter of a turn.

4 Knead by pushing down and away from you until the dough feels very smooth. It is better to make the dough in small batches (450 g/1 lb) for easier handling. Wrap in clingfilm and leave to rest for 20 minutes before rolling out and using.

To make wholewheat pasta, substitute the white flour with wholemeal strong flour. If you wish, you can use half durum wheat flour and half wholemeal flour. You may need a little extra oil to make a soft and pliable dough.

COLOURED AND FLAVOURED PASTA DOUGH

As well as being made in all kinds of shapes and sizes, pasta can also be made in a variety of different colours and flavours. Coloured, flavoured pastas provide an interesting and delicious change and are easily achieved.

SPINACH PASTA (PASTA VERDI)

Wash 225 g/8 oz fresh spinach thoroughly, discarding the tough stems and outer leaves. Place in a large pan with just the water that is left clinging to the leaves and cook for 3 minutes or until tender. Drain, squeezing out as much moisture as possible using absorbent kitchen paper, then chop very finely. Add to the eggs before the flour is mixed into the basic pasta dough. Extra flour can be added to absorb excess moisture.

SAFFRON PASTA

Infuse 1 teaspoon saffron strands in 1 teaspoon warm water for 15 minutes. Add to the eggs before the flour is mixed into the basic pasta dough.

TOMATO PASTA

Add 2–3 tablespoons tomato purée to the eggs before the flour is mixed into the basic pasta dough.

BLACK PASTA

Add 1 teaspoon squid ink to the eggs before the flour is mixed into the basic pasta dough. Take care not to use too much excess flour when making this pasta or the density of the colour will be lost.

MUSHROOM PASTA

Reconstitute 25 g/1 oz dried ceps in 3 tablespoons boiling water for at least 30 minutes. Thoroughly drain, squeezing out excess moisture with absorbent kitchen paper, and chop very finely. Add to the eggs before the flour is mixed into the basic pasta dough.

BEETROOT PASTA

Purée 25 g/1 oz fresh cooked beetroot and rub through a sieve to remove any lumps. Add to the eggs before the flour is mixed into the basic pasta dough. For a darker coloured pasta, use an extra 25 g/1 oz sieved beetroot.

HERB PASTA

Finely chop 3 tablespoons fresh herbs and mix into the eggs before the flour is mixed into the basic pasta dough. Try basil, oregano, sage, tarragon, mint or even a combination of two or three different herbs. For added flavour, add 1–2 crushed garlic cloves, 1 seeded and finely chopped chilli, or 1 tablespoon grated lemon zest.

CHOCOLATE PASTA

Melt 50 g/2 oz plain chocolate or very good dark chocolate in a bowl placed over a pan of gently simmering water, or use the microwave. Cool slightly and mix into the eggs. Add 2 tablespoons sifted unsweetened cocoa powder to the flour. Mix the melted chocolate into the basic pasta dough when the eggs are being added.

CITRUS PASTA

Add 2 tablespoons freshly grated lemon, lime or orange zest, or a mixture of all three zests to the eggs before the flour is mixed into the basic pasta dough.

HOW TO USE YOUR ROLLING AND CUTTING MACHINE

1 Clamp your machine securely onto the work surface and insert the handle. Turn the regulator knob so that it is at its widest setting. Wipe the machine thoroughly with a clean cloth (see also page 8).

2 Cut the prepared dough in half, flour lightly and feed each half through the rollers while turning the handle.

3 Sprinkle with a very light dusting of flour and fold in half. Press the seams together firmly with the heel of your hand.

4 Pass through the roller a further six to eight times, until the dough feels smooth and elastic, folding the dough in half and lightly dusting with flour after each time.

5 Decrease space between the rollers one notch at a time. Feed the dough through without folding in half. If it becomes unmanageable, cut it in half and cover one half with a teatowel while rolling the other half.

6 Lightly dust the dough with flour to prevent it sticking to the rollers. When the dough has reached the right thickness, cover with a clean teatowel and leave to dry for about 5–10 minutes before cutting.

CUTTING THE DOUGH

1 Attach the cutting head to the machine by sliding the attachments into the brackets on either side of the machine. Before you cut the pasta, it must feel dry so that the pasta does not stick to itself. Take care not to let it become too dry or brittle, however, as then it will not cut properly. Carefully pass the pasta through the cutting head, turning the handle at the same time.

2 When the cut pasta has reached the correct length, cut with a pair of scissors. Toss with a little flour.

3 If you are cooking the pasta within 1 hour, place flat on a clean teatowel. If you are keeping the pasta for longer, whether a few hours or days, wrap loosely round your hand to form small nests and place on a teatowel to dry. Store in an airtight jar.

MAKING RAVIOLI

Ravioli is easy to make when using your pasta machine. The ravioli attachment cuts three rows of mini filled cases of pasta. It can be stuffed with a variety of fillings, such as ricotta cheese, spinach or ham.

1 Prepare the dough as before and roll it until a long, thin sheet of pasta is achieved. Cut the sheet of pasta with the cutter enclosed with the ravioli attachment and dust with flour. Clamp the machine to the table and fix the ravioli attachment to the machine. Fold the sheet of pasta dough in half and insert the closed half into the plastic hopper of the ravioli attachment.

NOTE If you do not have the ravioli attachment for your machine, simply roll out the pasta dough as thinly as possible. Cut out 5–7.5 cm/ 2–3 inch squares or rounds with a pastry cutter. Place a spoonful of the filling in the centre, dampen the edges, and fold over to encase the filling. Pinch the edges firmly together. Dry for at least I hour on a floured plate.

2 Carefully separate the pasta and lay each sheet over the wooden roller of the hopper. Turn the handle slowly until the pasta has been caught by the rollers and the two pasta sheets sealed together.

3 Prepare the stuffing and use to fill the hopper. Turn the handle slowly and three rows of filled cases will appear. Repeat, filling the hopper with any remaining stuffing. Sprinkle with a little flour and leave the ravioli to dry for I hour before cutting.

USING A HAND-OPERATED EXTRUDER PASTA MACHINE

ifferent makes of machine vary so it is always advisable to check before buying your machine to ensure that it will give you the pasta you require.

Ensure you clean the machine well after use. Turn the handle in the opposite direction and remove the hopper. Loosen the closing ring nut with the wrench and remove the fork and cutter or die holder. Turn the chamber anticlockwise to remove the extruder parts. Completely remove all the pieces of the machine that are removable, wash in hot soapy water, dry well and reassemble after a few hours when the parts are completely dry. Any remaining pieces of pasta can be removed with a clean, dry brush.

Never wash your machine parts in a dishwasher.

1 Wipe the machine with a clean cloth. Clamp the machine securely to the work surface with the clamp provided and insert the handle in the SLOW opening. (The fast opening is used only for meat mincing and dough making.) Fit the die of the shape you wish to extrude.

Make the dough and leave to relax, wrapped in clingfilm. Place a small piece of dough into the hopper and slowly turn the handle.

2 After a few seconds the shapes will begin to come out of the die in the machine. When they have reached the required length, cut with a sharp knife. Repeat until all the pasta has been cut. If the pasta shapes are sticking together, sprinkle with a little flour. Leave to dry for about 1 hour before cooking.

3 To change the die, turn the turning handle a few times in the opposite direction and lift up and remove the hopper. Using the wrench, unscrew the closing ring nut. Choose the cutter or die you wish to use and place on the end of the extrusion barrel. Ensure that it fits correctly with the four tabs of the die engaged in the notches on the barrel. Screw the ring nut back, put the hopper back in place and begin to extrude your pasta.

MAKING PASTA SHAPES

If you do not have a machine which produces shaped pastas, or you want a pasta shape that cannot be made from a machine, below are instructions as to how you can make some of the most popular shapes by hand.

Brandelle Roll out the prepared dough and tear into pieces giving random shapes and sizes.

Garganelli Cut a 5 cm/2 in square of pasta, moisten one side with water, then roll at an angle around the handle of a wooden spoon. Allow to dry then remove from handle.

Farfalle Roll your prepared dough into a rectangle and divide into neat 5 cm/2 in squares. Using a serrated pastry cutter or wheel, divide the squares in half. Pinch the centre of each halved square to form a bow or butterfly shape.

Fusilli Cut 5 cm/2 in squares of pasta into four strips. Roll around a thick skewer to form a spiral. Lightly roll over a grooved wooden butter shaper, remove and allow to dry.

Maltagliati Roll out the pasta dough into a rectangle then cut out irregular shapes using a sharp knife or a plain or serrated pastry cutter.

Orecchiette Roll small pieces of dough into balls about 1–2.5 cm/ ½–1 in diameter. Press in the centre of each ball, allowing the pasta to curl upwards so there is a hollow in the centre.

COOKING AND SERVING PASTA

It is important for the greatest enjoyment of pasta that it is cooked correctly. "Al dente" is the classic Italian expression used to describe the texture of pasta when it is correctly cooked. It should still be slightly firm with a bite to it. The only way to check is by tasting. Simply remove a piece of the pasta from the saucepan and bite it; if it has a chewy feel, then it is ready. Fresh pasta such as angel hair can take as little as 30 seconds to cook; by the time the water has come back to the boil after the pasta has been added, it is virtually ready. Other fresh pasta can take 1–2 minutes, while lasagne sheets can take 3–4 minutes.

To test if filled pastas are cooked, taste the edge of the pasta rather than trying to cut through the stuffing.

Dried pasta takes longer to cook; again the best way to check is by tasting.

As a general rule, allow 4 litres/7 pints water to 450 g/1 lb pasta. Use a large saucepan which will enable the pasta to move around in the water. Bring the water to the boil before adding any salt or the pasta. Use 1 tablespoon salt for 450 g/ 1 lb pasta. Add the salt as the water comes to the boil, then add the pasta all at once.

NOTE It is a misconception that oil needs to be added to the water when cooking pasta. Cooking the pasta in plenty of water and stirring frequently just after the pasta has been added should prevent it from sticking together. The only exception is when cooking the large, flat ribbon pastas.

Immediately after the pasta has been added, stir to prevent it sticking to the pan. This will also help to submerge long strands of pasta. Put a lid on the pan to bring the water back to the boil as quickly as possible. Once the water has come back to the boil, remove the lid. Stir occasionally and taste until the pasta is cooked to "al dente."

Drain immediately through a colander and shake gently. Always save a little of the pasta cooking water; it is ideal for thinning down sauces if they are too thick. Do not rinse as this cools the pasta and removes the starch which makes the sauce stick to the pasta.

As a general rule, if serving pasta as an appetizer, allow 75–100 g/3–4 oz of fresh pasta per person. If it is served as a main meal with meat, fish, or vegetables in a sauce with a green salad, allow 100–150 g/4–5 oz of fresh pasta per serving.

The recipes serve six as starters and four when served as a main meal with a green salad and crusty bread. The desserts serve four.

NUTRITIONAL ANALYSIS

The analysis has been based upon each meal serving four people and it takes into account only the pasta dish itself and not any accompaniments that you may choose to serve with the meal.

The data box provides nutritional information per serving (a quarter of the recipe) so that you can see at a glance how many calories you will be having and how many grams of the macronutrients, carbohydrate, protein and total fat the serving contains. Using the nutrition facts you will also be able to see how much sugar, dietary fibre, salt and cholesterol you will be having together with a breakdown of the total fat into saturated, monosaturated and polyunsaturated fats.

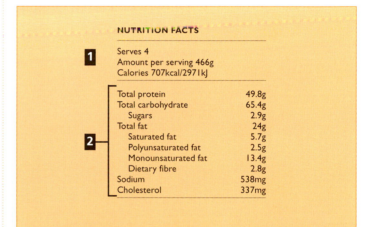

NUTRITION FACTS

1
Serves 4
Amount per serving 466g
Calories 707kcal/2971kJ

Total protein	49.8g
Total carbohydrate	65.4g
Sugars	2.9g
Total fat	24g
Saturated fat	5.7g
Polyunsaturated fat	2.5g
Monounsaturated fat	13.4g
Dietary fibre	2.8g
Sodium	538mg
Cholesterol	337mg

1 Serving size for one portion, in metric measure. Since the serving size is defined, it is easier to make a meaningful comparison of nutritional benefits.

2 Nutrients most important to health today.

CHAPTER THREE

CLASSIC SAUCES

Sauces play an integral part in the eating of pasta. A good sauce can often mean the difference between an indifferent meal and one of true gastronomic delight. The sauces in this chapter are traditional and are the most popular to serve with pasta. They can also be used in baked or filled pasta dishes.

SPICY TOMATO SAUCE

This sauce is made hot and spicy by the use of fresh jalapeño chillies. Dried crushed chillies can be substituted; use ¼–½ teaspoon depending on how hot you like it.

Makes 600 ml/1 pint

For the sauce
- 675 g/1½ lb fresh plum tomatoes
- 3 tbsp virgin olive oil
- 1-2 garlic cloves, peeled and crushed
- 1-2 jalapeño chillies, seeded and finely chopped
- 2 tbsp tomato purée
- 1 tbsp roughly chopped fresh oregano
- salt and ground black pepper

To serve
- 450 g/1 lb fresh pasta
- freshly grated Pecorino Romano cheese

Make a small cross in the top of each tomato and place in a large bowl. Cover with boiling water and leave for 2-3 minutes. Drain and peel. Cut into quarters, discard the seeds, then roughly chop the flesh.

Heat the oil in a pan and gently sauté the garlic and chillies for 3 minutes, taking care not to let the garlic or chillies burn. Add the chopped tomatoes and tomato purée blended with 2 tablespoons water. Bring to the boil, reduce the heat and simmer for 15 minutes or until a sauce consistency is reached. Add the chopped oregano with seasoning to taste and leave to simmer while you cook the pasta.

Cook the pasta in plenty of salted boiling water for 1-2 minutes or until "al dente." Drain and toss with the sauce. Serve immediately, handing the grated cheese separately.

NUTRITION FACTS

Serves 4
Amount per serving 322g
Calories 492kcal/2071kJ

Total protein	17.5g
Total carbohydrate	65.2g
Sugars	7.8g
Total fat	20g
Saturated fat	4.8g
Polyunsaturated fat	2.3g
Monounsaturated fat	11.2g
Dietary fibre	4.4g
Sodium	286mg
Cholesterol	186mg

PESTO

Perhaps one of the best-loved and well-known of all the sauces, now used in many other dishes as well as pasta. Originating in the Liguria region of Italy, where the Genoese grow the tiny sweet basil leaves to make their world-famous pesto.

Makes 225 ml/8 fl oz

NUTRITION FACTS

Serves 4
Amount per serving 180g
Calories 658kcal/2751kJ

Total protein	19.8g
Total carbohydrate	59.5g
Sugars	1,4g
Total fat	40g
Saturated fat	8.2g
Polyunsaturated fat	5.7g
Monounsaturated fat	23g
Dietary fibre	2.5g
Sodium	419mg
Cholesterol	193mg

For the sauce
◆ 50 g/2 oz fresh basil leaves
◆ 8 tbsp extra virgin olive oil
◆ 25 g/1 oz pine nuts
◆ 2-3 garlic cloves, peeled
◆ salt
◆ 50 g/2 oz freshly grated Parmesan cheese
◆ 1 tbsp freshly grated Pecorino Romano cheese

To serve
◆ 450 g/1 lb fresh pasta
◆ extra freshly grated Parmesan cheese
◆ fresh basil leaves

Place the fresh basil leaves, extra virgin olive oil, pine nuts and garlic in a food processor and blend the ingredients together until smooth. Spoon into a bowl and stir in salt to taste and the freshly grated cheeses.

Meanwhile, cook the pasta in plenty of salted boiling water for 1-2 minutes or until "al dente". Drain and toss with the pesto sauce. Serve immediately with extra freshly grated cheese and a few basil leaves to garnish.

CARBONARA

There are many different variations of this sauce, but they all use the same basic ingredients, although the proportions may vary. For those seeking a slightly healthier version of this classic sauce, omit the butter and increase the oil by 2 tablespoons, then substitute thick yogurt for the cream.

Makes 225 ml/8 fl oz

NUTRITION FACTS

Serves 4
Amount per serving 247g
Calories 674kcal/2821kJ

Total protein	25.6g
Total carbohydrate	62g
Sugars	4g
Total fat	38g
Saturated fat	15g
Polyunsaturated fat	2.9g
Monounsaturated fat	16.8g
Dietary fibre	2.7g
Sodium	937mg
Cholesterol	331mg

For the sauce

◆ 25 g/1 oz unsalted butter
◆ 3 tbsp olive oil
◆ 2-3 garlic cloves, peeled and crushed
◆ 1 large onion, peeled and finely chopped
◆ 100 g/4 oz pancetta or smoked lean bacon rashers, cut into thin strips
◆ 2 medium egg yolks
◆ 150 ml/¼ pt single cream
◆ 4 tbsp freshly grated Parmesan cheese
◆ salt and ground black pepper

To serve

◆ 450 g/1 lb fresh pasta
◆ 2 tbsp freshly grated Parmesan cheese
◆ chopped fresh flat leaf parsley

Heat the unsalted butter and oil in a pan and gently sauté the garlic and onion for 5 minutes or until softened but not browned. Add the pancetta or smoked bacon and continue to sauté for another 2 minutes.

Beat the egg yolks with the cream and 4 tablespoons of Parmesan, reserve.

Meanwhile, cook the pasta in plenty of salted boiling water for 1-2 minutes or until "al dente".

Drain thoroughly and return to the pan. Add the onion and pancetta mixture and heat through for 2 minutes stirring occasionally, then remove from the heat.

Add the egg and cream mixture and quickly mix together with two forks so that the eggs are cooked in the heat of the pasta. Season to taste and serve immediately with the Parmesan and sprinkle with chopped parsley.

FRESH TOMATO SAUCE

When making tomato sauce, look for tomatoes that are properly ripened but not over-ripe. For a true authentic taste, use plum tomatoes.

600 ml/1 pint

For the sauce
- 675 g/1½ lb tomatoes
- ½ small fennel bulb (about 2 tbsp chopped)
- 3 tbsp olive oil
- 1 onion, peeled and chopped
- 2-3 garlic cloves, peeled and crushed
- few sprigs of oregano
- 2-3 tbsp tomato purée
- 300 ml/½ pt vegetable stock
- salt and ground black pepper

To serve
- 450 g/1 lb fresh pasta
- 1-2 tsp chopped fresh oregano

Make a small cross in the top of each tomato and place in a large bowl. Cover with boiling water and leave for 2 minutes. Drain off the water and peel the tomatoes. Cut in half and chop roughly. Trim the fennel, discarding any damaged outer leaves, then chop finely.

Heat the oil in a pan and gently sauté the fennel, onion and garlic for 5 minutes or until soft but not browned. Add the chopped tomatoes with the oregano sprigs and continue to sauté for another 3 minutes.

Blend the tomato purée with a little of the vegetable stock, then add to the pan with the remaining stock. Bring to the boil and simmer for 10-12 minutes or until reduced to a sauce consistency. Remove the oregano sprigs and add seasoning to taste.

Meanwhile, cook the pasta in plenty of salted boiling water for 1-2 minutes or until "al dente". Drain the pasta thoroughly and add to the sauce with the chopped oregano. Toss lightly, then serve immediately.

CLAM AND CHILLI SAUCE

When cooking clams the same rule applies to clams as to mussels. Discard those that are open before cooking and those that remain closed after cooking.

Makes 475 ml/16 fl oz

For the sauce
- 900 g/2 lb fresh clams
- 4 tbsp olive oil
- 1 garlic clove, peeled and crushed
- 2 shallots, peeled and chopped
- 1 jalapeño chilli, seeded and finely chopped
- 300 ml/½ pt dry white wine
- salt and ground black pepper
- 4 tbsp single cream (optional)

To serve
- 450 g/1 lb fresh pasta
- 2 tbsp chopped fresh flat parsley

Scrub the clam shells and soak in cold water at least 30 minutes, discarding any that remain open. (If you tap an open clam before cooking and it closes, you can use it.) Drain the clams just before using.

Heat the oil in a large pan and gently saute the garlic, shallots and chilli for 5 minutes or until softened. Add the wine and simmer gently for 5 minutes.

Add the drained clams, cover with a lid and steam for 5 minutes or until all the clams have opened. Carefully shake the pan occasionally until the clams have opened. Discard any that remain closed. Remove from the heat and stir in the seasoning and cream.

Meanwhile, cook the pasta in plenty of salted boiling water for 1-2 minutes or until cooked to almost "al dente". Drain the pasta thoroughly and reserve.

Add the pasta to the clam pan and place over a medium heat. Continue to cook for 1-2 minutes or until the pasta has finished cooking. Remove from the heat and add the parsley. Stir and serve immediately.

NUTRITION FACTS

Serves 4
Amount per serving 466g
Calories 707kcal/2971kJ

Total protein	49.8g
Total carbohydrate	65.4g
Sugars	2.9g
Total fat	24g
Saturated fat	5.7g
Polyunsaturated fat	2.5g
Monounsaturated fat	13.4g
Dietary fibre	2.8g
Sodium	538mg
Cholesterol	337mg

SPRING VEGETABLE AND CREAM SAUCE

You can generally buy most vegetables all year round. However, when home-grown produce first comes into the stores or the new baby vegetables first appear, make the most of them and make this delicious sauce.

Makes 475 ml/16 fl oz

For the sauce
- 75 g/3 oz young asparagus, trimmed
- 75 g/3 oz new or baby carrots, trimmed
- 50 g/2 oz shelled broad beans
- 50 g/2 oz sugar snap peas
- 50 g/2 oz unsalted butter
- 2 shallots, peeled and chopped
- 75 g/3 oz courgettes, diced

- 200 ml/7 fl oz double cream
- salt and ground black pepper
- 4 tbsp freshly grated Parmesan cheese

To serve
- 450 g/1 lb fresh pasta
- sprig of opal basil

Cut the asparagus into short lengths. Blanch in lightly salted boiling water for 2 minutes. Drain and refresh in cold water, then drain again.

Slice long carrots or cut baby carrots in half. Cook in lightly salted boiling water for 2-3 minutes or until almost tender. Drain and refresh in cold water, then drain again. Blanch the broad beans for 3 minutes and the sugar snap peas for 1 minute. Refresh in cold water and drain.

Melt the unsalted butter in a large pan and gently sauté the shallots for 5 minutes. Add the courgettes and sauté for a further 1 minute. Add all the drained, refreshed vegetables to the double cream and cook gently, stirring, for about 5-8 minutes or until the cream has reduced slightly.

Meanwhile, cook the pasta in plenty of salted boiling water for 1-2 minutes or until "al dente". Drain thoroughly, then add to the vegetable and cream sauce. Add seasoning to taste with the grated cheese. Heat through gently for 1 minute. Garnish with a sprig of opal basil.

SUN-DRIED TOMATO AND BLACK OLIVE SAUCE

This is a robust sauce and is ideally suited to the thicker ribbons of pasta, such as tagliatelle, or shapes such as penne or garganelli.

Makes 225 ml/8 fl oz

For the sauce
◆ 2 tbsp olive oil
◆ 1 tbsp sun-dried tomato oil
◆ 8 sun-dried tomatoes in oil, finely chopped
◆ 1 medium onion, peeled and finely chopped
◆ 2 garlic cloves, peeled and crushed
◆ 2 celery stems, trimmed and finely chopped
◆ 50 g/2 oz pancetta, chopped
◆ 50 g/2 oz black olives, stoned and chopped

◆ 1 tbsp tomato purée
◆ 300 ml/½ pt vegetable stock
◆ few sprigs of marjoram
◆ salt and ground black pepper

To serve
◆ 450 g/1 lb fresh pasta
◆ extra sprigs marjoram
◆ freshly grated Parmesan cheese

Heat the olive oil and 1 tablespoon of the sun-dried tomato oil in a pan and sauté the onion, sun-dried tomatoes, garlic, celery and pancetta for 5 minutes. Stir in half the olives.

Blend the tomato purée with a little of the stock, then stir into the pan with the remaining stock and the marjoram. Bring to the boil and simmer for 10 minutes. Cool, then pass through

a food processor and return to the pan. Add seasoning to taste with the remaining olives. Cover with a lid and remove from the heat.

Meanwhile, cook the pasta in plenty of salted boiling water for 1-2 minutes or until "al dente". Drain well, then add the tomato sauce and toss lightly. Serve immediately, scattered with torn marjoram sprigs and Parmesan cheese.

QUICK TOMATO SAUCE

This sauce is ideal when time is critical and you are relying on store cupboard ingredients. It is also an excellent sauce to use for filled pasta as well as layered dishes.

Makes 225 ml/8 fl oz

NUTRITION FACTS

Serves 4
Amount per serving 253g
Calories 420kcal/1771kJ

Total protein	14g
Total carbohydrate	63.3g
Sugars	5.4g
Total fat	14.4g
Saturated fat	2.7g
Polyunsaturated fat	1.7g
Monounsaturated fat	8.3g
Dietary fibre	3.3g
Sodium	317mg
Cholesterol	178mg

For the sauce
◆ 2 tbsp olive oil
◆ 1 large onion, peeled and grated
◆ 400 g/14 oz can chopped tomatoes
◆ salt and ground black pepper
◆ few dashes Tabasco sauce

To serve
◆ 450 g/1 lb fresh pasta
◆ freshly shaved Parmesan cheese

Heat the oil in a large pan and sauté the onion for 5 minutes. Add the contents of the can of tomatoes and sauté gently for 10 minutes. Add seasoning and Tabasco sauce to taste, cover with a lid and remove from the heat.

Meanwhile, cook the pasta in plenty of boiling water for 1-2 minutes or until "al dente". Drain thoroughly, then return to the pan. Add the tomato sauce to the cooked pasta. Heat through for 2 minutes, tossing lightly, then serve immediately, sprinkled with fresh shavings of Parmesan cheese.

GARLIC AND OLIVE OIL SAUCE

One of the simplest of sauces yet one of the most delicious. As with good wines, the better the olive oil used the better the taste, so don't skimp on the quality of the oil.

Makes 150 ml/¼ pint

<table>
<tr><td colspan="2">NUTRITION FACTS</td></tr>
<tr><td colspan="2">Serves 4</td></tr>
<tr><td colspan="2">Amount per serving 147g</td></tr>
<tr><td colspan="2">Calories 522kcal/2187kJ</td></tr>
<tr><td>Total protein</td><td>13g</td></tr>
<tr><td>Total carbohydrate</td><td>58.8g</td></tr>
<tr><td>Sugars</td><td>1.2g</td></tr>
<tr><td>Total fat</td><td>28g</td></tr>
<tr><td>Saturated fat</td><td>4.6g</td></tr>
<tr><td>Polyunsaturated fat</td><td>2.8g</td></tr>
<tr><td>Monounsaturated fat</td><td>18.4g</td></tr>
<tr><td>Dietary fibre</td><td>2.5g</td></tr>
<tr><td>Sodium</td><td>263mg</td></tr>
<tr><td>Cholesterol</td><td>178mg</td></tr>
</table>

For the sauce

◆ 2-4 garlic cloves, peeled
◆ 6-8 tbsp extra virgin olive oil
◆ salt and ground black pepper
◆ 1 tbsp roughly chopped fresh flat leaf parsley

To serve

◆ 450 g/1 lb fresh pasta

Finely chop the garlic. Place in a pan with the oil and sauté gently for 5 minutes. Add seasoning to taste with the parsley, cover the pan with a lid and remove from the heat.

Meanwhile, cook the pasta in plenty of salted boiling water for 1-2 minutes or until "al dente". Drain and add the garlic sauce. Toss lightly, then serve immediately.

RAGU

This sauce is native to the Italian city of Bologna. There, every family has its own recipe, which has been passed down through the generations.

Makes 475 ml/16 fl oz

For the sauce
- 2 tbsp olive oil
- 2-4 garlic cloves, peeled and crushed
- 1 onion, peeled and finely chopped
- 2 celery stems, trimmed and finely chopped
- 1 large carrot, peeled and diced
- 350 g/12 oz lean minced beef
- 225 ml/8 fl oz dry white wine
- 400 g/14 oz can chopped tomatoes
- 1 tbsp tomato purée
- salt and ground black pepper
- 1 tbsp chopped fresh oregano

To serve
- 450 g/1 lb fresh pasta
- freshly grated Parmesan cheese

Heat the olive oil in a large pan and sauté the garlic, onion, celery stems and diced carrot for 5-8 minutes or until softened but not browned. Add the beef and continue to sauté for 5 minutes or until sealed, stirring frequently to break up any lumps.

Add the wine and the contents of the can of tomatoes. Blend the tomato purée with 2 tablespoons water and stir into the pan. Bring to the boil, cover with a lid, then simmer for 20 minutes or until a thick consistency is reached. Add seasoning to taste with the chopped oregano, cover with a lid and remove from the heat. Reserve.

Meanwhile, cook the pasta in plenty of boiling salted water for 1-2 minutes or until "al dente". Drain thoroughly and return to the pan. Add the sauce and toss lightly. Either stir in the grated Parmesan cheese or pass the cheese separately. Serve immediately.

BUTTER AND TOMATO SAUCE

Always use unsalted butter when cooking, as it imparts a far better flavour.
You can also control the salt content far better.

Makes 475 ml/16 fl oz

For the sauce
◆ 675 g/1½ lb ripe beefsteak tomatoes, peeled
◆ 75 g/3 oz unsalted butter
◆ 6 shallots, peeled and finely chopped
◆ 3 tbsp fresh basil leaves
◆ salt and ground black pepper

To serve
◆ 450 g/1 lb fresh pasta
◆ basil leaves
◆ freshly grated Parmesan cheese

NUTRITION FACTS

Serves 4
Amount per serving 347g
Calories 546kcal/2294kJ

Total protein	16.4g
Total carbohydrate	65.9g
Sugars	8g
Total fat	26.2g
Saturated fat	13.3g
Polyunsaturated fat	2.1g
Monounsaturated fat	8.7g
Dietary fibre	4.4g
Sodium	474mg
Cholesterol	227mg

Seed and dice the tomatoes. Melt 4 tablespoons of butter in a large pan and gently sauté the shallots for 5 minutes or until softened. Add the remaining butter and the tomatoes and continue to sauté gently for 5-8 minutes or until the tomatoes have begun to break down. Stir in the basil leaves with seasoning to taste. Cover with a lid and remove from the heat.

Meanwhile, cook the pasta in plenty of salted boiling water for 1-2 minutes or until "al dente". Drain thoroughly and add to the tomato sauce. Toss lightly and serve immediately, garnished with extra basil leaves. Hand some freshly grated Parmesan cheese separately.

CHAPTER FOUR

PASTA SHAPES

It is very easy to make all kinds of shapes with the pasta that you have made using your machine. Just turn to the front of the book to see how to cut them once you have made the basic dough. Some pasta shapes are better suited to certain dishes than others, so think about the sauce you are serving.

Garganelli with Chicken

I am a great lover of dried apricots and the addition of apricots here gives this dish an added dimension.

For the sauce
- 225 g/8 oz boneless, skinless chicken breasts
- 4 tbsp olive oil
- 2 garlic cloves, peeled and cut into thin slivers
- 1 red onion, peeled and sliced into thin wedges
- 1 orange pepper, seeded and thinly sliced
- 50 g/2 oz chopped ready-to-eat dried apricots
- 1 tbsp chopped fresh rosemary
- 4 tbsp dry white wine
- salt and ground black pepper

To serve
- 450 g/1 lb fresh garganelli
- freshly shaved Pecorino Romano cheese

Discard any sinews from the chicken and cut into thin strips. Heat the oil in a frying pan and sauté the garlic and onion for 5 minutes or until softened. Add the chicken and continue to sauté, stirring, for 3 minutes, or until the chicken is completely sealed.

Add the pepper, apricots and rosemary and cook for 1 minute, then add the wine with seasoning to taste. Bring to the boil, cover with a lid and simmer for 3-4 minutes or until the chicken is cooked. Remove from the heat.

Meanwhile, cook the garganelli in plenty of boiling salted water for 1-2 minutes or until "al dente". Drain, reserving 2 tablespoons of the pasta cooking liquor. Return the pasta and liquor to the pan with the cooked chicken mixture and toss lightly. Serve immediately with the freshly shaved cheese.

NUTRITION FACTS

Serves 4
Amount per serving 280g
Calories 558kcal/2346kJ

Total protein	27.5g
Total carbohydrate	68.1g
Sugars	10.3g
Total fat	20.5g
Saturated fat	3.6g
Polyunsaturated fat	2.3g
Monounsaturated fat	12.6g
Dietary fibre	4.1g
Sodium	302mg
Cholesterol	218mg

Maltagliati with Ceps

Fresh ceps are very hard to find especially outside of Italy. Look for dried ceps, choosing those packages where you can easily see that you are buying the mushroom not just the stem. Remember that they will need soaking for at least 30 minutes before use.

For the sauce
- 25 g/1 oz dried ceps
- 6 tbsp virgin olive oil
- 4 smoked garlic cloves, peeled and thinly sliced
- 1 tbsp chopped fresh rosemary
- 1 tbsp chopped fresh sage
- 175 g/6 oz mushrooms, trimmed and sliced
- 4 tbsp dry white wine
- 225 g/8 oz green beans, trimmed, sliced and blanched

To serve
- 450 g/1 lb fresh maltagliati
- freshly shaved Pecorino Romano cheese
- sprigs of rosemary and sage

Soak the ceps in warm water for about 30 minutes. Drain, chop into small pieces and reserve. Heat the oil in a pan and sauté the garlic for 2 minutes. Stir in the chopped herbs, ceps and mushrooms and continue to sauté for 4 minutes. Add the wine and green beans, then bring to the boil. Reduce the heat, cover with a lid and simmer for 3 minutes.

Meanwhile, cook the maltagliati in plenty of salted boiling water for 1-2 minutes or until "al dente". Drain and return to the pan. Add the sauce to the pasta and toss lightly. Serve immediately, topped with the freshly shaved cheese and sage and rosemary sprigs to garnish.

NUTRITION FACTS

Serves 4
Amount per serving 270g
Calories 560kcal/2347kJ

Total protein	18.2g
Total carbohydrate	61.3g
Sugars	2.9g
Total fat	27.8g
Saturated fat	5.5g
Polyunsaturated fat	3.2g
Monounsaturated fat	16.9g
Dietary fibre	5g
Sodium	226mg
Cholesterol	183mg

Pasta and Ratatouille

Ratatouille is a classic Mediterranean dish; combine it with pasta and you have an all-time favourite. I have used canned tomatoes in this recipe but if you prefer you can use 675 g/1¹/₂ lb fresh peeled tomatoes and an extra tablespoon of tomato purée.

NUTRITION FACTS

Serves 4
Amount per serving 453g
Calories 491kcal/2071kJ

Total protein	17.9g
Total carbohydrate	67.4g
Sugars	10.8g
Total fat	17g
Saturated fat	4.4g
Polyunsaturated fat	1.9g
Monounsaturated fat	9.3g
Dietary fibre	5.6g
Sodium	316mg
Cholesterol	12mg

For the sauce
- 1 medium aubergine, trimmed and sliced
- salt
- 4 tbsp olive oil
- 1 large onion, peeled and thinly sliced
- 2-4 garlic cloves, peeled and chopped
- 175 g/6 oz sliced courgettes
- 2 × 400 g/14 oz cans chopped tomatoes
- 1 tbsp tomato purée

- 6 tbsp red wine
- ground black pepper
- 1 tbsp chopped fresh oregano
- 1 tbsp chopped fresh flat leaf parsley
- 75 g/3 oz button mushrooms, wiped and halved

To serve
- 300 g/10 oz fresh orecchiette
- 75 g/3 oz mozzarella cheese, sliced

Layer the aubergine in a colander, sprinkling between each layer with salt. Leave for 30 minutes. Drain, rinse well in cold water and pat dry.

Heat the oil in a large pan and sauté the aubergine, onion, garlic and courgettes for 5-8 minutes or until softened. (You may need to add a little more olive oil as the aubergine will tend to soak it up.)

Add the tomatoes. Blend the tomato purée with the wine and stir into the pan with the black pepper, oregano, parsley and mushrooms.

Bring to the boil, reduce the heat, cover with a lid and simmer for 15 minutes or until the vegetables are tender but still retain a bite.

Meanwhile, cook the orecchiette in plenty of boiling salted water for 1-2 minutes or until "al dente". Drain and place in the base of an ovenproof gratin dish.

Pour over the prepared sauce and top with the sliced mozzarella cheese. Place under a medium hot grill and cook for 5-8 minutes or until the cheese has melted and is golden.

Pasta and Ratatouille

Farfalle with Salmon

Farfalle with Salmon

This is certainly one of my favourite recipes and is one that I inevitably fall back on when I have friends visit. It works equally well either as a starter or as a main meal if served with plenty of crusty bread and salad.

For the sauce
- 175 g/6 oz broccoli florets
- 4 tbsp butter
- 225 g/8 oz leeks, thinly sliced
- 4 plum tomatoes, peeled, seeded and chopped
- 150 ml/¼ pt double cream
- 225 g/8 oz smoked salmon, cut into thin strips

To serve
- 450 g/1 lb fresh farfalle
- ground black pepper

Divide the broccoli into tiny florets, then blanch in boiling water for 2 minutes. Drain and refresh in cold water. Reserve.

Melt the butter in a pan and sauté the leeks for 4 minutes, stirring frequently. Add the drained broccoli and tomatoes, cream and smoked salmon and heat through, stirring occasionally. Cover with a lid and reserve.

Meanwhile, cook the farfalle in plenty of salted boiling water for 1-2 minutes or until "al dente". Drain and return to the pan. Add the cream and smoked salmon mixture. Toss lightly and serve immediately sprinkled with freshly ground black pepper.

NUTRITION FACTS

Serves 4
Amount per serving 432g
Calories 749kcal/3136kJ

Total protein	31g
Total carbohydrate	65.2g
Sugars	7.4g
Total fat	42.6g
Saturated fat	22g
Polyunsaturated fat	3.5g
Monounsaturated fat	13.7g
Dietary fibre	6.1g
Sodium	1363mg
Cholesterol	281mg

Garganelli with Eggplants

Aubergines come in many different shapes. There seems to be a growing trend to discard the idea of sprinkling the aubergine with salt prior to cooking and with the baby aubergine it certainly does not seem to be necessary.

For the sauce
- 6 tbsp olive oil
- 3 garlic cloves, peeled and thinly sliced
- 4 shallots, peeled and cut into thin wedges
- 4–5 baby aubergines, cut into small strips
- 1 small red pepper, seeded and chopped
- 1 small green pepper, seeded and chopped
- 2 × 400 g/14 oz can chopped tomatoes
- 1 tbsp chopped fresh rosemary
- salt and ground black pepper

To serve
- 450 g/1 lb fresh garganelli
- freshly grated Parmesan cheese

Heat the olive oil in a large pan and gently sauté the garlic, shallots and aubergine strips for 10 minutes or until softened. Add the peppers and sauté for a further 2 minutes, then add the chopped tomatoes, rosemary and seasoning to taste. Bring to the boil, reduce the heat and simmer for 5-8 minutes or until a thick sauce consistency is reached.

Cook the garganelli in plenty of salted boiling water for 1-2 minutes or until "al dente". Drain and return to the pan. Add the aubergines and tomato sauce. Toss lightly and serve immediately with the grated cheese.

NUTRITION FACTS

Serves 4
Amount per serving 528g
Calories 588kcal/2469kJ

Total protein	18.6g
Total carbohydrate	71.2g
Sugars	12.4g
Total fat	27.7g
Saturated fat	5.4g
Polyunsaturated fat	3g
Monounsaturated fat	16.8g
Dietary fibre	7.1g
Sodium	400mg
Cholesterol	183mg

ORECCHIETTE WITH HERBS

*You can vary the herbs that you use according to availability and personal taste.
The flavour will be better if you finely chop the herbs rather than blending them to
a paste in a food processor.*

NUTRITION FACTS

Serves 4
Amount per serving 160g
Calories 549kcal/2299kJ

Total protein	15.8g
Total carbohydrate	58.9g
Sugars	1.4g
Total fat	29.7g
Saturated fat	11.8g
Polyunsaturated fat	4.5g
Monounsaturated fat	11.1g
Dietary fibre	2.5g
Sodium	332mg
Cholesterol	218mg

For the sauce
◆ 4 tbsp butter
◆ 2 garlic cloves, peeled and finely chopped
◆ 6 tbsp chopped fresh mixed herbs, such as basil, oregano, flat leaf parsley, chives, rosemary and sage
◆ grated zest and juice of 1 lemon
◆ 25 g/1 oz toasted pine nuts
◆ 1 tbsp extra virgin olive oil

Melt the butter in a pan and sauté the garlic for 3 minutes. Add the herbs and lemon zest and juice and continue to sauté for 2 minutes. Stir in the toasted pine nuts.

Meanwhile, cook the orecchiette in plenty of salted boiling water for 1-2 minutes or until "al dente". Drain, reserving 2 tablespoons of the cooking liquor.

To serve
◆ 450 g/1 lb fresh orecchiette
◆ freshly shaved Parmesan cheese

Return the pasta to the pan with the cooking liquor and add the herb sauce and olive oil. Toss lightly and serve immediately with the freshly shaved Parmesan cheese.

BRANDELLE GENOESE

*This sauce will work as well with any of the prepared home-made unfilled pastas
as with ravioli or tortelloni.*

NUTRITION FACTS

Serves 4
Amount per serving 344g
Calories 545kcal/2288kJ

Total protein	20.4g
Total carbohydrate	64.8g
Sugars	6.6g
Total fat	24.9g
Saturated fat	5.4g
Polyunsaturated fat	2.6g
Monounsaturated fat	14.3g
Dietary fibre	3.8g
Sodium	419mg
Cholesterol	302mg

For the sauce
◆ 4 tbsp olive oil
◆ 1 large onion, peeled and chopped
◆ 2 garlic cloves, peeled and finely chopped
◆ 600 ml/1 pt passata
◆ 1 tbsp roughly torn fresh basil
◆ salt and ground black pepper
◆ 2 medium eggs, beaten

Heat the oil in a large pan and sauté the onion and garlic for 8 minutes or until very soft. Pour in the passata and bring to the boil. Reduce the heat and simmer for 10 minutes. Add the basil leaves and seasoning to taste.

Meanwhile, cook the brandelle in plenty of salted boiling water for 1-2 minutes or until "al dente". Drain.

To serve
◆ 450 g/1 lb fresh brandelle
◆ 50 g/2 oz freshly grated Parmesan cheese

Gently reheat the sauce and, without allowing the sauce to boil, whisk in the eggs. Cook gently, whisking throughout until the sauce thickens. Add the pasta and Parmesan cheese, toss lightly and serve immediately.

Orecchiette with Herbs

MALTAGLIATI WITH LAMB AND CHIVES

If preferred you can use minced lamb, but I prefer to buy leg of lamb and chop the meat very finely.

For the sauce
◆ 3 tbsp olive oil
◆ 2 garlic cloves, peeled and finely chopped
◆ 1 large onion, peeled and chopped
◆ 300 g/10 oz lean lamb, trimmed and finely chopped
◆ 400 g/14 oz can chopped tomatoes
◆ 1 tbsp tomato purée

◆ 4 tbsp red wine
◆ 1 tbsp snipped fresh chives
◆ salt and ground black pepper

To serve
◆ 450 g/1 lb fresh maltagliati
◆ 2-3 tbsp freshly grated Parmesan cheese
◆ extra snipped fresh chives

Heat the oil in a pan and sauté the garlic and onion for 5 minutes or until softened. Add the lamb and continue to sauté for 5 minutes, stirring frequently, until browned.

Add the chopped tomatoes, the tomato purée blended with 2 tablespoons water and the red wine. Bring to the boil, reduce the heat, cover with a lid and simmer for 40 minutes or until a thick sauce is formed. Add the snipped chives and seasoning to taste and continue to simmer for 5 minutes while cooking the pasta.

Cook the pasta in plenty of salted boiling water for 1-2 minutes or until "al dente". Drain and return to the pan. Add the meat sauce, toss lightly, then serve sprinkled with the grated Parmesan cheese and extra snipped fresh chives.

MALTAGLIATI WITH ASPARAGUS AND BABY CORN

Maltagliati means torn or badly cut, so its shape works well with asparagus and baby corn after they have been cut into shorter lengths. For vegetarians, just leave out the Parma ham and add a few extra toasted pine nuts.

For the sauce
◆ 25 g/1 oz butter
◆ 1 white onion, peeled and thinly sliced
◆ 8–10 asparagus spears, trimmed, woody part discarded and cut into 5 cm/2 in lengths
◆ 100 g/4 oz baby corn, cut into 5 cm/2 in lengths
◆ 200 ml/7 fl oz double cream
◆ 25 g/1 oz toasted pine nuts

◆ 1 tbsp chopped fresh basil
◆ 75 g/3 oz Parma ham, shredded
◆ salt and ground black pepper
◆ 25 g/1 oz freshly grated Parmesan cheese

To serve
◆ 450 g/1 lb fresh maltagliati

Melt the butter in a pan and gently sauté the onion for 5 minutes or until softened. Add the asparagus spears and continue to sauté for 2 minutes, then add the corn and cream.

Bring the cream mixture to the boil, reduce the heat and simmer for 2 minutes. Stir in the pine nuts, basil, Parma ham, seasoning to taste and cheese. Heat through, stirring, then cover with a lid and remove from the heat.

Meanwhile, cook the fresh maltagliati in plenty of salted boiling water for 1-2 minutes or until "al dente". Drain and return to the pan. Add the sauce to the pasta, toss lightly, then serve immediately.

Maltagliati with Lamb and Chives

Macaroni with Peppers, Chillies and Opal Basil

MACARONI WITH PEPPERS, CHILLIES AND OPAL BASIL

When using chillies take care as their heat level can be deceptive. Remove the seeds as well as the membrane that the seeds are attached to. As a general guide, remember, the smaller the chilli the hotter the heat level.

For the sauce
- 2 red peppers, seeded
- 2 yellow peppers, seeded
- 2 green peppers, seeded
- 1-3 jalapeño chillies, seeded
- 4 tbsp olive oil
- 1 large onion, peeled and finely sliced
- 3 smoked garlic cloves, peeled and finely sliced
- 475 ml/16 fl oz passata
- salt and ground black pepper
- few sprigs of opal basil

To serve
- 450 g/1 lb fresh macaroni
- sprigs of opal basil
- freshly grated Pecorino Romano cheese

Heat the grill to high then chargrill the peppers and chillies for 10 minutes or until the skins have blistered. Remove from the heat and place in a plastic bag until cool. Then, peel and cut into thin strips.

Heat the oil in a large pan and sauté the onion and garlic for 5 minutes or until softened. Add the peppers with the passata and bring to the boil. Cover with a lid, reduce the heat and simmer for 5-8 minutes or until the sauce has thickened. Add the seasoning to taste and the basil sprigs.

Meanwhile, cook the macaroni in plenty of salted boiling water for 1-2 minutes or until "al dente". Drain and return to the pan. Add the prepared sauce and toss lightly. Serve immediately garnished with the opal basil sprigs and hand the grated cheese separately.

NUTRITION FACTS

Serves 4
Amount per serving 514g
Calories 553kcal/2326kJ

Total protein	18.7g
Total carbohydrate	74.8g
Sugars	16g
Total fat	22.2g
Saturated fat	4.6g
Polyunsaturated fat	2.6g
Monounsaturated fat	12.8g
Dietary fibre	7g
Sodium	374mg
Cholesterol	183mg

FARFALLE WITH MORTADELLA

One tip that I learnt early on when cooking pasta is to save some of the pasta cooking liquor. It is the best way to moisten the pasta or to thin the sauce if it has become too thick. So when draining the cooked pasta, always keep a little until you have served the dish.

For the sauce
- 3 tbsp olive oil
- 225 g/8 oz leeks, sliced
- 2-3 garlic cloves, peeled and cut into thin slivers
- 400 g/14 oz can chopped tomatoes
- 150 ml/¼ pt red wine
- 175 g/6oz mortadella, sliced and cut into thin strips
- 2 tbsp chopped fresh flat leaf parsley

To serve
- 450 g/1 lb fresh farfalle

Heat the oil in a pan and sauté the leeks and garlic for 5 minutes. Add the contents of the can of tomatoes and the red wine.

Bring to the boil, reduce the heat and cover with a lid. Simmer for 10 minutes or until the sauce has been reduced by about half or until a thick consistency is reached. Add the strips of mortadella to the sauce and simmer gently while cooking the pasta.

Cook the farfalle in plenty of boiling salted water for 1-2 minutes or until "al dente". Drain and return to the pan. Add the sauce and parsley, then toss lightly. Serve immediately, handing the grated cheese separately.

NUTRITION FACTS

Serves 4
Amount per serving 374g
Calories 597kcal/2506kJ

Total protein	21.2g
Total carbohydrate	64g
Sugars	5.4g
Total fat	27.7g
Saturated fat	7g
Polyunsaturated fat	3.1g
Monounsaturated fat	15.3g
Dietary fibre	4.6g
Sodium	685mg
Cholesterol	205mg

MALTAGLIATI WITH ANCHOVIES

When using anchovies, soak in a little milk for about 30 minutes before using, then drain and pat dry. This removes any excess salt and helps provide the healthier diet that is so desirable today. The colour and delicious taste combinations of this simple dish make it very appealing.

NUTRITION FACTS

Serves 4
Amount per serving 286g
Calories 557kcal/2339kJ

Total protein	26g
Total carbohydrate	67.8g
Sugars	5g
Total fat	22.4g
Saturated fat	3.9g
Polyunsaturated fat	2.7g
Monounsaturated fat	11.2g
Dietary fibre	6.6g
Sodium	1225mg
Cholesterol	183mg

For the sauce
◆ 225 g/8 oz mangetout
◆ 3 tbsp olive oil
◆ 1 red onion, peeled and finely sliced
◆ 2 garlic cloves, peeled and finely chopped
◆ 100 g/4 oz sliced Parma ham, cut into thin strips
◆ 175 g/6 oz green cabbage, finely shredded

◆ 50 g/2 oz can anchovy fillets, drained and soaked in milk for 30 minutes
◆ salt and ground black pepper

To serve
◆ 450 g/1 lb fresh maltagliati
◆ freshly shaved Pecorino Romano cheese

Cook the mangetout in lightly salted boiling water for 2-3 minutes or until tender, drain and reserve. Heat the oil in a pan and sauté the onion and garlic for 5 minutes or until softened. Add the mangetout, ham and cabbage and continue to sauté for a further 3 minutes.

Meanwhile, cook the pasta in plenty of salted boiling water for 1-2 minutes or until "al dente". Drain, reserving 4 tablespoons of the liquor.

Add the pasta liquor to the onion, mangetout and ham mixture together with the anchovy fillets and seasoning to taste. Add the cooked pasta to the mixture. Toss lightly before serving with the freshly shaved cheese.

ORECCHIETTE WITH SAUSAGE AND PANCETTA

Pancetta is cured in the same way as prosciutto but is not matured for as long and is generally unsmoked. If you can not find pancetta, use smoked bacon.

NUTRITION FACTS

Serves 4
Amount per serving 512g
Calories 774kcal/3240kJ

Total protein	25.5g
Total carbohydrate	71.6g
Sugars	9.3g
Total fat	39.6g
Saturated fat	16.5g
Polyunsaturated fat	4.1g
Monounsaturated fat	16.1g
Dietary fibre	4.9g
Sodium	1177mg
Cholesterol	238mg

For the sauce
◆ 50 g/2 oz butter
◆ 1 onion, peeled and sliced
◆ 100 g/4 oz pancetta, thinly chopped
◆ 225 g/8 oz pork sausages, skinned
◆ 300 ml/½ pt red wine
◆ few sprigs sage

◆ 8 plum tomatoes, peeled, seeded and chopped
◆ ¼ tsp freshly grated nutmeg

To serve
◆ 450 g/1 lb fresh orecchiette
◆ freshly grated Parmesan cheese

Melt the butter in a pan and sauté the onion and pancetta for 5 minutes or until the onion has softened and the pancetta has become golden. Roll the sausage into small balls. Add to the pan and sauté for 5 minutes or until browned. Add the wine, sage and tomatoes. Bring to the boil, cover with a lid and simmer for 5 minutes, stirring occasionally.

Meanwhile, cook the orecchiette in plenty of salted boiling water for 1-2 minutes or until "al dente". Drain and return to the pan. Add the nutmeg to the sauce and pour over the pasta. Toss lightly and serve immediately sprinkled with the cheese.

Maltagliati with Anchovies

Beef Stew with Pasta

Beef Stew with Pasta

This recipe is based on the Corsican Stufatu, *but I have added a few extra ingredients to make it a hearty and filling dish.*

For the sauce
- 2 tbsp olive oil
- 1 large onion, peeled and chopped
- 2-3 garlic cloves, peeled and crushed
- 450 g/1 lb chuck steak, trimmed and diced
- 2 tbsp seasoned flour
- 150 ml/¼ pt red wine
- 475 ml/16 fl oz beef stock
- salt and ground black pepper

- 2 tbsp chopped fresh oregano
- 4–6 baby carrots, trimmed
- 225 g/8 oz leeks, blanched and sliced

To serve
- 300 g/10 oz fresh fusilli
- freshly grated Parmesan cheese
- chopped fresh oregano

Preheat the oven to 180°C/350°F/Gas mark 4, 10 minutes before cooking the stew. Heat the oil in a large pan and sauté the onion and garlic for 5 minutes or until softened but not browned.

Toss the meat in the seasoned flour, then add to the pan and brown, stirring frequently. Sprinkle in any remaining flour and cook for 2 minutes. Gradually stir in the wine and stock. Bring to a boil, stirring, then remove from the heat and stir in seasoning to taste and the

oregano. Pour into a casserole dish, cover with a lid, and cook for 1½ hours.

Cut the carrots in half if large. Cook in boiling water for 3 minutes, drain, and add to the stew with the leeks. Continue to cook for 30 minutes or until the meat is tender.

Meanwhile, cook the fusilli in plenty of salted boiling water for 1-2 minutes or until "al dente". Drain and stir into the stew. Sprinkle with the grated Parmesan and oregano and serve.

NUTRITION FACTS

Serves 4
Amount per serving 429g
Calories 598kcal/2524kJ

Total protein	39.6g
Total carbohydrate	74.5g
Sugars	10g
Total fat	15.35g
Saturated fat	4.7g
Polyunsaturated fat	2g
Monounsaturated fat	7.2g
Dietary fibre	6.7g
Sodium	531mg
Cholesterol	70mg

Brandelle with Ceps and Anchovies

As this is based on the famous pesto sauce, treat it in exactly the same way. Store in the refrigerator in a screw top jar. Dispel any air bubbles and cover with a thin layer of olive oil. Consume within 24 hours.

For the sauce
- 15 g/½ oz dried ceps
- 6-8 tbsp olive oil
- 2 firm tomatoes, peeled, seeded and chopped
- 50 g/2 oz pine nuts
- 4 garlic cloves
- small bunch basil leaves

- 4 anchovy fillets, soaked in milk for 30 minutes, chopped

To serve
- 450 g/1 lb fresh brandelle
- freshly shaved Parmesan cheese

Soak the ceps in warm water for about 30 minutes. Drain, reserving the soaking liquor and chop the ceps. Heat 2 tablespoons of the oil in a pan and gently sauté the ceps for 2 minutes. Strain the soaking liquid, then add to the ceps and cook until the liquid has almost evaporated. Add the tomatoes and heat for 1 minute.

Place the mushroom mixture with the pine nuts, garlic, basil leaves and anchovies in a food

processor. Blend for 1 minute. With the motor still running, gradually pour in the remaining oil until a thick paste is formed.

Meanwhile, cook the brandelle in plenty of salted boiling water for 1-2 minutes or until "al dente". Drain and return to the pan. Add the mushroom paste and toss lightly until the pasta is coated. Serve immediately sprinkled with the shaved Parmesan.

NUTRITION FACTS

Serves 4
Amount per serving 216g
Calories 650kcal/2715kJ

Total protein	18.4g
Total carbohydrate	60.8g
Sugars	3.1g
Total fat	38.9g
Saturated fat	5.3g
Polyunsaturated fat	8.2g
Monounsaturated fat	20.9g
Dietary fibre	3.6g
Sodium	564mg
Cholesterol	178mg

PASTA LAMB BAKE

This dish can be made ahead of time and cooked later. If doing this, I would recommend that you make the sauce slightly thinner as, while it sits, the pasta will soak up more of the sauce than if you cook it immediately.

NUTRITION FACTS

Serves 4
Amount per serving 273g
Calories 520kcal/2169kJ

Total protein	17.3g
Total carbohydrate	35.4g
Sugars	5g
Total fat	32.6g
Saturated fat	5.9g
Polyunsaturated fat	11.9g
Monounsaturated fat	12.8g
Dietary fibre	2g
Sodium	620mg
Cholesterol	42mg

For the sauce
◆ 225 g/8 oz lean lamb, trimmed and diced
◆ 2 tbsp olive oil
◆ 1 onion, peeled and chopped
◆ 2 garlic cloves, peeled and crushed
◆ 8 sun-dried tomatoes, chopped
◆ 1 red pepper, seeded and chopped

◆ 150 ml/¼ pt red wine
◆ 300 ml/½ pt passata
◆ 1 tbsp chopped fresh oregano
◆ salt and ground black pepper

To serve
◆ 225 g/8 oz fresh farfalle
◆ 75 g/3 oz mozzarella cheese, grated

Preheat the oven to 190°C/375°F/Gas mark 5, 10 minutes before baking the pasta dish.

Heat the oil in a frying pan and sauté the onion, garlic, sun-dried tomatoes and red pepper for 5 minutes or until softened. Add the lamb and sauté for a further 3 minutes or until sealed. Add the red wine, passata and oregano with seasoning to taste. Simmer for 5 minutes, then remove from the heat.

Meanwhile, cook the farfalle in plenty of salted boiling water for 1 minute or until almost "al dente". Drain and return to the pan. Add the lamb and sauce and toss lightly.

Spoon the mixture into an ovenproof dish and top with the grated mozzarella cheese. Bake the pasta dish in the preheated oven for 20 minutes or until the cheese has melted and is golden and bubbly.

FARFALLE WITH TURKEY AND CEPS

Turkey is traditionally reserved for special occasions, which seems a great shame. As turkey is so low in fat, we really should be eating more of it.

NUTRITION FACTS

Serves 4
Amount per serving 320g
Calories 527kcal/2216kJ

Total protein	29.1g
Total carbohydrate	62.5g
Sugars	4.8g
Total fat	18.2g
Saturated fat	3.4g
Polyunsaturated fat	2.5g
Monounsaturated fat	10.5g
Dietary fibre	4.8g
Sodium	300mg
Cholesterol	210mg

For the sauce
◆ 25 g/1 oz dried ceps
◆ 1 red pepper, seeded
◆ 1 green pepper, seeded
◆ 3 tbsp olive oil
◆ 2 garlic cloves, peeled and thinly sliced
◆ 225 g/8 oz turkey breast meat, trimmed and thinly sliced

◆ 100 g/4 oz button mushrooms, wiped and sliced
◆ 6 tbsp dry white wine
◆ salt and ground black pepper
◆ 2 tbsp chopped fresh flat leaf parsley

To serve
◆ 450 g/1 lb fresh farfalle
◆ freshly shaved Parmesan cheese

Soak the porcini in warm water for about 30 minutes. Drain, chop finely, and reserve.

Preheat the broiler to high, then charbroil the peppers for 10 minutes or until the skins have blistered. Remove from the heat; place in a plastic bag until cool. Skin and cut into thin strips.

Heat the oil in a pan and sauté the garlic and turkey for 5 minutes or until the turkey is sealed. Add the chopped ceps and button mushrooms and continue to sauté for 3 more minutes.

Add the pepper strips and wine to the pan and simmer for 5 minutes. Stir in the seasoning to taste and chopped parsley. Cover with a lid and remove from the heat while cooking the fresh farfalle.

Cook the farfalle in plenty of salted boiling water for 1-2 minutes or until "al dente". Drain and place on a warm serving plate. Top with the reserved turkey mixture and serve sprinkled with the shaved cheese.

Pasta Lamb Bake

Angel Hair with Tuna and Olives

ANGEL HAIR WITH TUNA AND OLIVES

When black olives are used in a recipe you will often find capers, too. For a far superior flavour, look for capers that have been preserved in salt rather than vinegar or brine, then soak them in cold water for at least 30 minutes before use.

For the sauce
- 4 tbsp olive oil
- 2 leeks, trimmed and thinly sliced
- 1-2 smoked garlic cloves, peeled and finely chopped
- 400 g/14 oz can chopped tomatoes
- 1-2 tbsp tomato purée
- 2 × 200 g/7 oz cans tuna, drained

- 50 g/2 oz black olives, halved and stoned
- 2 tbsp capers
- salt and ground black pepper

To serve
- 450 g/1 lb fresh angel hair pasta
- fresh sprigs of basil

Heat the oil in a pan and sauté the leeks and garlic for 5 minutes or until softened but not browned. Add the contents of the can of tomatoes and the tomato purée blended with 150 ml/¼ pt water. Bring to the boil, cover with a lid and simmer for 10 minutes or until a thick sauce consistency is reached. Add the tuna, olives, capers and seasoning to taste. Heat through gently for 5 minutes.

Meanwhile, cook the angel hair pasta in plenty of salted boiling water for 1-2 minutes or until "al dente". Drain well and return to the pan. Add the sauce to the pasta and toss lightly. Serve immediately, garnished with the basil sprigs.

NUTRITION FACTS

Serves 4
Amount per serving 396g
Calories 589kcal/2480kJ

Total protein	38.5g
Total carbohydrate	63.7g
Sugars	5.9g
Total fat	22g
Saturated fat	3.9g
Polyunsaturated fat	2.6g
Monounsaturated fat	13.2g
Dietary fibre	4.5g
Sodium	922mg
Cholesterol	229mg

FETTUCCINE WITH MEAT SAUCE

There are many different variations to the classic Bolognese meat sauce; all are equally delicious. I especially like this recipe as the pancetta adds to the flavour.

For the sauce
- 4 tbsp olive oil
- 1 onion, peeled and finely chopped
- 1 celery stick, trimmed and finely chopped
- 1 carrot, peeled and finely diced
- 50 g/2 oz pancetta, thinly sliced and diced
- 300 g/10 oz lean minced beef
- 150 ml/¼ pt red wine

- 150 ml/¼ pt beef stock
- salt and ground black pepper
- 1 tbsp chopped fresh marjoram

To serve
- 450 g/1 lb fresh fettuccine
- freshly grated Pecorino Romano cheese

Heat the oil in a pan and sauté the onion, celery, carrot and pancetta for 5-8 minutes or until softened but not browned. Add the beef and continue to sauté, stirring frequently to break up any lumps, for 5 minutes or until sealed.

Add the wine, stock, seasoning and marjoram. Bring to the boil, reduce the heat and simmer, stirring occasionally, for 12-15 minutes or until the sauce has thickened.

Meanwhile, cook the fettuccine in plenty of salted boiling water for 1-2 minutes or until "al dente". Drain and return to the pan. Add the sauce, toss lightly and serve immediately, handing the grated cheese separately.

NUTRITION FACTS

Serves 4
Amount per serving 323g
Calories 660kcal/2769kJ

Total protein	34.5g
Total carbohydrate	62.4g
Sugars	4.5g
Total fat	29.8g
Saturated fat	8g
Polyunsaturated fat	2.7g
Monounsaturated fat	16.3g
Dietary fibre	3.4g
Sodium	889mg
Cholesterol	228mg

ANGEL HAIR PASTA WITH SCALLOPS

Because angel hair pasta and scallops need so little cooking, this dish is quickly prepared; it is ready in about 5 minutes.

NUTRITION FACTS

Serves 4
Amount per serving 307g
Calories 764kcal/3197kJ

Total protein	32.3g
Total carbohydrate	64g
Sugars	4g
Total fat	44.1g
Saturated fat	24g
Polyunsaturated fat	2.6g
Monounsaturated fat	13.9g
Dietary fibre	3g
Sodium	512mg
Cholesterol	307mg

For the sauce
- 50 g/2 oz butter
- 12 large scallops, cleaned and halved, corals removed if preferred
- 8 spring onions, trimmed and diagonally sliced
- 100 g/4 oz sugar snap peas, trimmed and halved

- salt and dash of cayenne pepper
- 200 ml/7 fl oz double cream

To serve
- 450 g/1 lb fresh angel hair pasta
- paprika

Melt the butter in a pan and sauté the scallops for 3 minutes, stirring frequently. Add the spring onions and continue to sauté for 1 minute. Add the sugar snap peas and cook for 1 minute. Season to taste. Pour in the cream and simmer gently while cooking the pasta.

Cook the angel hair pasta in plenty of salted boiling water for 1 minute or until "al dente". Drain and return to the pan. Add the scallop and cream mixture and toss lightly. Serve immediately sprinkled with a little paprika.

ANGEL HAIR PASTA WITH TRUFFLES AND MUSHROOMS

The best truffles are the white ones found in Alba in Piedmont and are available fresh between October to January. Black truffles are found extensively in Umbria and Perigord in France and are used mainly for cooking, as the flavour is not as intense as the white truffle. If white truffle is unavailable, use the black truffle and 1 teaspoon truffle oil.

NUTRITION FACTS

Serves 4
Amount per serving 288g
Calories 603kcal/2522kJ

Total protein	16.6g
Total carbohydrate	61.8g
Sugars	3.7g
Total fat	34.1g
Saturated fat	17.8g
Polyunsaturated fat	2.4g
Monounsaturated fat	11g
Dietary fibre	4.2g
Sodium	409mg
Cholesterol	246mg

For the sauce
- 25 g/1 oz dried ceps
- 50 g/2 oz butter
- 2-3 smoked garlic cloves, peeled and chopped
- 1 onion, peeled and chopped
- 350 g/12 oz mixed mushrooms, such as field, button and oyster

- 4 tbsp double cream
- salt and ground black pepper
- 1 tbsp chopped fresh flat leaf parsley

To serve
- 450 g/1 lb fresh angel hair pasta
- 25 g/1 oz white truffle, shaved

Soak the ceps in warm water for 30 minutes. Drain and reserve. Heat the butter in a pan and sauté the garlic and onion until softened.

Wipe and roughly chop the mushrooms, then add to the pan with the ceps. Continue to sauté for 5-8 minutes or until the mushrooms have softened. Stir in the cream, seasoning to taste and parsley.

Heat for 1 minute, then cover with a lid and remove from the heat.

Cook the angel hair pasta in plenty of salted boiling water for 1 minute. Drain well, then return to the pan.

Pour over the mushroom sauce. Toss lightly, then serve immediately sprinkled with the shaved truffle.

Angel Hair Pasta with Scallops

Spaghettini with Leeks and Onions

SPAGHETTINI WITH LEEKS AND ONIONS

I particularly like the flavour of red onions as they have a much sweeter flavour than brown onions. Their colour complements the green of the leek.

For the sauce
- 4 tbsp olive oil
- 1 large red onion, peeled and cut into wedges
- 2–3 young leeks, trimmed and sliced
- 4 shallots, peeled and cut into thin slivers
- 2 × 400 g/14oz cans chopped tomatoes
- salt and ground black pepper
- 2 tbsp chopped fresh flat leaf parsley

To serve
- 450 g/1 lb fresh spaghettini
- 4-6 tbsp freshly grated Parmesan cheese

Heat the oil in a frying pan and gently sauté the onion for 5 minutes. Add the leeks and shallots and continue to sauté for 3 more minutes. Add the chopped tomatoes with seasoning to taste and simmer gently for 5-8 minutes or until the sauce has been reduced by about half.

Meanwhile, cook the spaghettini in plenty of salted boiling water for 1-2 minutes or until "al dente". Drain thoroughly and return to the pan. Add the sauce to the pan with the chopped parsley and toss lightly. Serve immediately, handing the cheese separately.

NUTRITION FACTS

Serves 4
Amount per serving 438g
Calories 543kcal/2285kJ

Total protein	19.6g
Total carbohydrate	69.2g
Sugars	10.3g
Total fat	23.1g
Saturated fat	5.3g
Polyunsaturated fat	2.4g
Monounsaturated fat	13.2g
Dietary fibre	5.5g
Sodium	439mg
Cholesterol	187mg

FETTUCCINE WITH CHICKEN LIVERS AND MUSHROOMS

Chicken livers are often used in Italian sauces. Here, they have been combined with wild mushrooms to make a particularly tasty dish.

For the sauce
- 25 g/1 oz dried ceps
- 4 tbsp olive oil
- 2–3 leeks, trimmed and sliced
- 175 g/6 oz chanterelle mushrooms
- 225 g/8 oz chicken livers
- 3 tbsp dry sherry
- 1 tbsp tomato purée
- 5 tbsp chicken stock
- salt and ground black pepper

To serve
- 450 g/1 lb fresh fettuccine
- freshly shaved Pecorino Romano cheese

Soak the ceps in warm water for 30 minutes, drain and reserve ceps and liquid.

Heat the oil in a frying pan and sauté the leeks for 2 minutes. Add the ceps and chanterelle mushrooms and sauté for 3 minutes. Drain and set to one side.

Clean the chicken livers and cut into thin strips. Add to the pan and quickly seal, stirring. Return the mushrooms to the pan and add the cep soaking liquid and sherry. Blend the tomato purée with the stock and seasoning to taste. Stir into the pan. Bring to the boil and simmer for 5 minutes or until a sauce consistency is reached.

Meanwhile, cook the fettuccine in plenty of salted boiling water for 1-2 minutes or until "al dente". Drain and return to the pan. Add the sauce and toss lightly. Serve with the freshly shaved cheese.

NUTRITION FACTS

Serves 4
Amount per serving 309g
Calories 542kcal/2277kJ

Total protein	26.1g
Total carbohydrate	61.1g
Sugars	3.4g
Total fat	22g
Saturated fat	4g
Polyunsaturated fat	2.8g
Monounsaturated fat	12.6g
Dietary fibre	4.4g
Sodium	642mg
Cholesterol	392mg

TAGLIATELLE WITH MEATBALLS

These tiny meatballs would be ideal to serve with any of the long ribbon pastas.
They would also work equally well with farfalle or fusilli.

For the sauce
- 1 small onion, peeled and finely chopped
- 1-2 garlic cloves, peeled and minced
- 225 g/8 oz lean minced lamb
- salt and ground black pepper
- 1 tbsp grated lemon zest
- 25 g/1 oz fresh white breadcrumbs
- 1 tbsp chopped fresh marjoram
- 1 tbsp pine nuts, toasted and chopped
- 1 medium egg, beaten

- 1-2 tbsp olive oil
- 300 ml/½ pt passata
- 150 ml/¼ pt red wine
- few sprigs of marjoram

To serve
- 450 g/1 lb fresh tagliatelle
- freshly grated Parmesan cheese
- marjoram sprig

Place the onion, garlic, lamb, seasoning, lemon zest, breadcrumbs, chopped marjoram and pine nuts in a bowl and mix well. Bind together with the egg. Dampen your hands, then form the mixture into tiny balls, each about the size of a cherry.

Heat the olive oil in a pan and brown the meatballs on all sides. Remove from the pan and wipe the pan clean. Add the passata, red wine and marjoram sprigs to the pan and bring to the boil. Boil for 5 minutes, reduce the heat and add the meatballs. Cover with a lid and simmer gently for 5-8 minutes or until the meatballs are cooked.

Meanwhile, cook the tagliatelle in plenty of salted boiling water for 1-2 minutes or until "al dente". Drain and place on a warm serving platter. Discard the marjoram sprigs from the sauce, then spoon the sauce and meatballs over the tagliatelle. Serve with the grated cheese and garnish with a marjoram sprig.

Tagliatelle with Meatballs

Tagliatelle with Seafood

TAGLIATELLE WITH SEAFOOD

The choice of fish is entirely up to you, but bear in mind the varying flavours and textures of the different fish you put together. If you have difficulty obtaining saffron threads, a tiny dash of turmeric will give the distinctive yellow colour but the flavour will be impaired.

For the sauce
- 350 g/12 oz assorted fresh fish fillets, such as salmon, trout, cod or haddock, skinned
- 15 g/½ oz butter
- 225 g/8 oz leeks, thinly sliced
- 100 g/4 oz button mushrooms, trimmed and sliced
- few strands of saffron
- 5 tbsp dry white wine
- 4 tbsp double cream

To serve
- 450 g/1 lb fresh tagliatelle
- few sprigs of flat leaf parsley

Cut the fish into small cubes, discarding any small bones that may remain after filleting. Heat the butter in a large pan and sauté the leeks and mushrooms for 3 minutes. Add the fish fillets and continue to sauté for another 3 minutes or until sealed. Sprinkle in the saffron, cook for 1 minute, then add the wine. Bring to the boil, cover with a lid, then simmer for 3-4 minutes or until the fish is cooked.

Meanwhile, cook the tagliatelle in plenty of salted boiling water for 3-4 minutes or until "al dente". Drain and return to the pan. Add the fish and cream to the pasta. Toss lightly and garnish with sprigs of flat leaf parsley. Serve immediately.

NUTRITION FACTS

Serves 4
Amount per serving 345g
Calories 644kcal/2701kJ

Total protein	32.1g
Total carbohydrate	60.9g
Sugars	3.3g
Total fat	30.8g
Saturated fat	13.8g
Polyunsaturated fat	3.2g
Monounsaturated fat	10.9g
Dietary fibre	3.8g
Sodium	421mg
Cholesterol	263mg

TRENETTE WITH ROCKET AND RADICCHIO

Many of us have only recently discovered the delights of both rocket and radicchio, but they are ingredients that are used regularly in many Italian dishes.

For the sauce
- 4 tbsp olive oil
- 4 shallots, peeled and sliced
- 100 g/4 oz prosciutto, thinly sliced into strips
- 400 g/14 oz can artichoke hearts, drained and quartered
- 3 tbsp vegetable stock
- 1 small head radicchio, thinly sliced
- salt and ground black pepper
- 1 tbsp balsamic vinegar
- 100 g/4 oz rocket

To serve
- 450 g/1 lb fresh trenette

Heat the oil in a pan and sauté the shallots and prosciutto for 5 minutes or until softened. Add the artichoke hearts, then stir in the stock and bring to the boil. Simmer for 2 minutes or until the liquid has reduced slightly.

Add the radicchio and simmer for 3 minutes or until the radicchio has softened. Season to taste. Cover with a lid and remove from the heat.

Meanwhile, cook the trenette in plenty of salted boiling water for 1-2 minutes or until "al dente". Drain and return to the pan. Add the radicchio mixture to the pan together with the balsamic vinegar and rocket. Toss lightly and serve immediately.

NUTRITION FACTS

Serves 4
Amount per serving 360g
Calories 522kcal/2197kJ

Total protein	21.8g
Total carbohydrate	64.1g
Sugars	4.9g
Total fat	22.5g
Saturated fat	4.3g
Polyunsaturated fat	2.7g
Monounsaturated fat	13.1g
Dietary fibre	3.3g
Sodium	1042mg
Cholesterol	183mg

CHAPTER SIX

FILLED PASTA

This chapter features classic dishes such as cannelloni, lasagne and ravioli. There are endless combinations that can be used with these pastas and whether it is fish, meat or vegetables, all of them are served with a sauce. Remember that the sauce needs to complement the pasta, not overwhelm its taste and texture.

WHOLEWHEAT LASAGNE WITH MEDITERRANEAN VEGETABLES

With the greater emphasis on healthy eating, more people are adopting the Mediterranean way of eating. With their vast array of sun-ripened vegetables, delicious pastas, breads and rich unctuous oils, it is easy to see why. Try this recipe, which captures this richness.

- 3 tbsp olive oil
- 1 onion, peeled and chopped
- 3 garlic cloves, peeled and crushed
- 6 sun-dried tomatoes, chopped
- 225 g/8 oz aubergines, chopped
- 1 yellow pepper, seeded and chopped
- 1 red pepper, seeded and chopped
- 225 g/8 oz courgettes, chopped

- 475 ml/16 fl oz passata
- 150 ml/¼ pt red wine
- salt and ground black pepper
- 1 tbsp chopped fresh oregano
- 6-8 fresh wholewheat lasagne sheets
- 4 firm tomatoes, sliced
- 50 g/2 oz mozzarella cheese, grated
- extra chopped fresh oregano

Preheat the oven to 190°C/375°F/Gas mark 5, 10 minutes before baking the lasagne. Heat the oil in a frying pan and sauté the onion, garlic and sun-dried tomatoes for 5 minutes. Add the aubergines, yellow and red peppers and courgettes, and continue to sauté for 3 more minutes.

Stir in the passata, wine, seasoning to taste and the oregano. Bring to the boil, reduce the heat and simmer for 15 minutes or until the vegetables are almost cooked.

Bring a large pan of water to the boil, add 1 tablespoon salt, then drop in four lasagne sheets, one at a time. Cook for 2-3 minutes, ensuring that they do not stick together. Drain, lay them on clean teatowels and pat dry. Repeat with the remaining lasagne sheets.

Place a layer of the vegetable sauce in the base of an ovenproof dish and top with half the lasagne sheets. Cover with the remaining sauce and then the lasagne sheets.

Arrange the tomato slices on top and sprinkle with the grated cheese. Bake in the oven for 25 minutes or until the cheese is golden and brown. Serve sprinkled with chopped oregano.

NUTRITION FACTS

Serves 4
Amount per serving 580g
Calories 609kcal/2571kJ

Total protein	19.9g
Total carbohydrate	90.1g
Sugars	17g
Total fat	18.6g
Saturated fat	3.7g
Polyunsaturated fat	3.7g
Monounsaturated fat	8.2g
Dietary fibre	8g
Sodium	336mg
Cholesterol	8mg

SEAFOOD LASAGNE

Traditionally, everyone thinks of lasagne with a ragu sauce, but in my opinion this version is one of the most delicious of all pasta recipes. You can vary the fish used according to availability and personal choice.

NUTRITION FACTS

Serves 4
Amount per serving 558g
Calories 695kcal/2935kJ

Total protein	51.3g
Total carbohydrate	87.2g
Sugars	14.6g
Total fat	18.1g
Saturated fat	9.9g
Polyunsaturated fat	1.2g
Monounsaturated fat	4.1g
Dietary fibre	5.1g
Sodium	969mg
Cholesterol	176mg

- ◆ 225 g/8 oz white fish fillets, such as cod
- ◆ 225 g/8 oz smoked haddock fillet or similar smoked fish
- ◆ 600 ml/1 pt skimmed milk
- ◆ 2-3 bay leaves
- ◆ 1 small onion, sliced
- ◆ few sprigs of parsley
- ◆ 50 g/2 oz butter or margarine
- ◆ 50 g/2 oz plain flour
- ◆ 1 tsp wholegrain mustard
- ◆ 25 g/1 oz grated hard cheese, such as mature Cheddar or Gruyère
- ◆ salt and ground black pepper
- ◆ 175 g/6 oz peeled prawns, thawed if frozen
- ◆ 100 g/4 oz tiny broccoli florets, blanched
- ◆ 6-8 fresh lasagne sheets
- ◆ 4 firm tomatoes, sliced
- ◆ 25 g/1 oz freshly grated Parmesan cheese

Preheat the oven to 190°C/375°F/Gas mark 5, 10 minutes before baking the lasagne. Wipe the fish and skin, discarding any bones. Place in a frying pan with 300 ml/½ pt of the milk, the bay leaves, onion and parsley. Place over a gentle heat and bring to the boil. Simmer for 8 minutes or until the fish is just cooked. Drain, reserving the milk; flake the fish and reserve.

For the white sauce, melt the butter or margarine in a small pan and stir in the flour. Cook, stirring, for 2 minutes. Remove from the heat and gradually stir in both amounts of reserved milk. Return to the heat and cook, stirring throughout, until the sauce thickens. Remove from the heat and stir in the mustard, grated cheese and seasoning to taste. Stir until the cheese has melted.

Squeeze out any excess moisture from the prawns and add to the flaked fish with the blanched broccoli.

Bring a large pan of water to the boil, add 1 tablespoon salt, then drop in four lasagne sheets, one at a time. Cook for 2-3 minutes, ensuring that they do not stick together. Drain, lay them on clean teatowels and pat dry. Repeat with the remaining lasagne sheets.

Spoon about a quarter of the prepared sauce into the base of an ovenproof dish and top with 3-4 sheets of lasagne. Cover this with half the fish and broccoli mixture and spoon over a further quarter of the sauce.

Repeat the layers, finishing with the lasagne sheets. Arrange the sliced tomatoes on top. Spoon over the remaining sauce and sprinkle with the grated Parmesan cheese. Bake the lasagne in the oven for 25 minutes or until golden brown and bubbly.

Seafood Lasagne

HAM, TOMATO AND MOZZARELLA RAVIOLI

The combinations for ravioli are endless, so instead of using the traditional meat filling, experiment with your favourite ingredients.

- 100 g/4 oz ricotta cheese
- 225 g/8 oz mozzarella cheese, thinly sliced
- 100 g/4 oz smoked ham, thinly sliced and cut into thin strips
- 2 firm tomatoes, peeled, seeded and chopped
- salt and ground black pepper
- 1 tbsp wholegrain mustard
- batch basic pasta dough (see page 20)
- 50 g/2 oz butter
- 1 tbsp chopped fresh sage

Place cheeses, smoked ham, tomatoes, seasoning and 1 teaspoon of the mustard in a mixing bowl, mix well and reserve.

Roll the pasta dough out and proceed to make the ravioli as previously described (see page 24). Repeat until all the filling and pasta has been used. Leave to dry for 1 hour before separating the squares.

Cook the ravioli in plenty of salted boiling water for 4-5 minutes or until "al dente". Drain and return to the pan. Add the remaining mustard, the butter and sage and toss lightly until the butter has melted and the ravioli is lightly coated. Serve immediately.

SPINACH, MUSHROOM AND RICOTTA CANNELLONI

The combination of spinach and ricotta cheese is superb and this filling would work equally well for either ravioli or lasagne.

- 1 tbsp olive oil
- 1 small onion, peeled and finely chopped
- 75 g/3 oz mushrooms, finely chopped
- 225 g/8 oz ricotta cheese
- 225 g/8 oz thawed frozen spinach
- salt and ground black pepper
- ½-1 tsp freshly grated nutmeg
- 12-14 fresh lasagne sheets
- Quick Tomato Sauce (see page 36)
- 50 g/2 oz mozzarella cheese, grated

Preheat the oven to 190°C/375°F/Gas mark 5, 10 minutes before baking the cannelloni. Heat the oil in a small pan and sauté the onion and mushrooms for 5 minutes. Drain and reserve.

Beat the ricotta cheese until soft and creamy, then beat in the drained onion mixture. Squeeze out any excess moisture from the spinach and beat into the cheese mixture together with seasoning to taste and the grated nutmeg.

Bring a large pan of water to a boil, add 1 tablespoon salt then drop in four lasagne sheets, one at a time. Cook for 1-2 minutes, ensuring that they do not stick together. Drain, lay them on clean teatowels and pat dry. Repeat with the remaining lasagne sheets.

Place about 2 tablespoons of the prepared filling at one end of a lasagne sheet. Moisten the edges and roll up to encase the filling. Dampen the edge to seal.

Place the filled tubes, seam side down, into the base of an ovenproof dish. Pour over the Quick Tomato Sauce. Sprinkle with the cheese. Bake the cannelloni in the oven for 25 minutes or until golden and bubbly.

VEGETABLE LASAGNE

There are many different fillings that can be used for lasagne. With the abundance of vegetables so readily available it would not be difficult to create a different lasagne for every day of the week.

- 50 g/2 oz butter or margarine
- 50 g/2 oz plain flour
- 475 ml/16 fl oz milk
- salt and ground black pepper
- 175 g/6 oz carrots, peeled and sliced into half moon shapes
- 100 g/4 oz shelled broad beans
- 100 g/4 oz green beans, trimmed and cut into 5 cm/2 in lengths
- 100 g/4 oz baby cauliflower florets

- 400 g/14 oz can red kidney beans, drained and rinsed
- 175 g/6 oz frozen spinach, thawed and chopped
- 50 g/2 oz Cheddar cheese, grated
- 1 tsp wholegrain mustard
- 6-8 fresh lasagne sheets
- 4 firm tomatoes, sliced
- 3 medium eggs
- 150 ml/¼ pt thick yogurt

Preheat the oven to 190°C/375°F/Gas mark 5, 10 minutes before baking the lasagne. Melt the butter or margarine in a small pan and stir in the flour. Cook over a gentle heat for 2 minutes then draw off the heat and gradually stir in the milk. Return the pan to the heat and cook, stirring until smooth, thick and glossy. Season and remove the pan from the heat. Cover with a sheet of dampened greaseproof paper and reserve.

Cook the carrots in lightly salted boiling water for 5 minutes or until just tender. Drain and reserve. Blanch the broad beans, green beans and cauliflower for 3 minutes. Drain and refresh in cold water. Mix with the carrots and kidney beans.

Squeeze out any excess moisture from the spinach, then beat into the prepared white sauce

with the cheese, seasoning to taste and the mustard. Place over a gentle heat and stir until smooth.

Bring a large pan of water to the boil, add 1 tablespoon salt, then drop in four lasagne sheets, one at a time. Cook for 2-3 minutes, ensuring that they do not stick together. Drain, lay them on clean teatowels, and pat dry. Repeat with the remaining lasagne sheets.

Place half the sauce and vegetables in the base of an ovenproof dish and cover with 3-4 lasagne sheets. Repeat once more, finishing with the pasta. Arrange the tomato slices on top. Beat the eggs with the yogurt, then pour over the tomatoes.

Bake the lasagne in the oven for 25-30 minutes or until the top is golden brown and bubbly. Serve.

NUTRITION FACTS

Serves 4
Amount per serving 690g
Calories 799kcal/3367kJ

Total protein	39.1g
Total carbohydrate	114.1g
Sugars	24g
Total fat	24g
Saturated fat	11.6g
Polyunsaturated fat	2.3g
Monounsaturated fat	6.4g
Dietary fibre	15.5g
Sodium	987mg
Cholesterol	224mg

Tortelloni with Parma Ham

TORTELLONI WITH PARMA HAM

Tortelloni take a little time and practise to make, but do persevere as they are well worth that extra bit of effort and are far superior to shop-bought ones. To begin with, use a simple sauce as used here, then as you get more proficient you can try different sauce and filling combinations.

- 1-2 tsp butter
- 2 small onions, peeled and finely chopped
- 50 g/2 oz mushrooms, finely chopped
- 225 g/8 oz ricotta cheese
- 50 g/2 oz Gruyère cheese, grated
- 100 g/4 oz Parma ham, trimmed and finely
- shredded

- batch basic pasta dough (see page 20)
- 1 tsp olive oil
- 4 spring onions, trimmed and finely chopped
- 400 g/14 oz can chopped tomatoes
- salt and ground black pepper
- 2 tbsp chopped fresh flat leaf parsley
  freshly grated Parmesan cheese

NUTRITION FACTS

Serves 4
Amount per serving 381g
Calories 603kcal/2533kJ

Total protein	30.3g
Total carbohydrate	65.2g
Sugars	7.1g
Total fat	26.7g
Saturated fat	12.2g
Polyunsaturated fat	2.1g
Monounsaturated fat	9.6g
Dietary fibre	3.8g
Sodium	995mg
Cholesterol	237mg

For the filling, melt the butter in a small pan and gently sauté one onion for 3 minutes. Add the mushrooms and continue to sauté for a further 3 minutes or until the mushrooms are lightly cooked. Drain and reserve.

Beat the ricotta cheese until creamy. Beat in the Gruyère cheese, the drained mushrooms and ham. Mix together.

Make the dough and roll out into long, thin sheets about 10 cm/4 in wide (see page 22).

Place the filling in a large piping bag and pipe small rounds of the filling onto one half of the dough. Brush the dough with a little water and fold over to completely encase the filling.

Cut into squares using a fluted biscuit cutter, making sure each square contains filling.

Moisten the edges and fold each square in half to form a triangle, pinching the edges together.

Pull the two corners together, wrapping them round the tip of your finger. Pinch the corners together on the seam. Repeat until all the triangles have been formed.

Cook the tortelloni in plenty of salted boiling water for 4-5 minutes. Drain and transfer to a serving dish.

While cooking the tortelloni, make the sauce. Heat the oil and gently sauté the other onion and spring onions for 2 minutes. Add the contents of the can of tomatoes and simmer for 5 minutes. Add seasoning to taste and the chopped parsley. Pour over the cooked tortelloni and serve with grated Parmesan cheese.

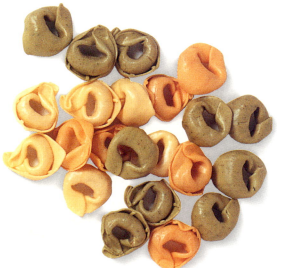

EASY-OVER RAVIOLI

This recipe takes the idea of ravioli but it is designed for those of us who have hectic lives. You can try the recipe with a variety of fillings. I have used minced chicken, but it would work equally well with minced lamb, beef or pork.

- 2 tbsp olive oil
- 1 jalapeño chilli, seeded and finely chopped
- 6 spring onions, trimmed and finely chopped
- 225 g/8 oz minced chicken
- 25 g/1 oz toasted and chopped pine nuts
- 50 g/2 oz fresh white breadcrumbs
- 25 g/1 oz ready-to-eat dried apricots, finely chopped
- 1 medium egg, beaten
- batch basic pasta dough (see page 20)
- Spicy Tomato Sauce (see page 29)
- few sprigs flat leaf parsley

Heat 1 tablespoon oil in a pan and sauté the chilli for 2 minutes. Add the spring onions and sauté for 1 more minute.

Add the chicken and sauté for 5 minutes or until cooked. Stir in the pine nuts, breadcrumbs and apricots, mixing well. Remove from the heat and add the egg to the mixture. Bind together. Return to the heat and cook gently for 2 minutes or until completely cooked. Keep warm.

Meanwhile, roll out the pasta dough and cut into 7.5 cm/3 in squares. Bring a large pan of water to the boil and add 1 tablespoon oil. Add the pasta squares one at a time and cook for about 3-4 minutes. Carefully remove and keep warm between clean, warm teatowels.

Reheat the tomato sauce, stirring occasionally. Place 2-3 cooked pasta squares onto warm plates. Top with a spoonful or two of the chicken mixture and cover with a further layer of pasta. Drizzle over a little tomato sauce and hand the remaining sauce separately. Garnish with flat leaf parsley sprigs.

TORTELLONI WITH RICOTTA AND HERBS

You can vary the herbs you use according to personal preference and availability. If liked, you can also use chopped spinach or even rocket.

- 225 g/8 oz ricotta
- 50 g/2 oz fontina, finely chopped
- 4 tbsp chopped fresh mixed herbs, such as basil, sage, flat leaf parsley and oregano
- 1 medium egg yolk
- salt and ground black pepper
- ½ tsp grated nutmeg
- batch basic pasta dough (see page 20)
- Butter and Tomato Sauce (see page 39)
- freshly grated Parmesan cheese
- extra 2 tbsp chopped fresh herbs to serve

For the filling, mix the cheeses with the 4 tablespoons chopped herbs, egg yolk, seasoning and nutmeg in a bowl. Roll out the pasta to 10 cm/4 in wide strips.

Place the filling in a piping bag and pipe small rounds onto one half of each strip. Moisten the edges and fold the dough over to completely encase the filling. Cut out into squares and proceed to form the tortelloni as previously described on page 83.

Cook the tortelloni in plenty of salted boiling water for 4-5 minutes or until "al dente". Drain and return to the pan.

Gently heat the sauce then pour over the cooked tortelloni. Toss lightly until coated. Serve immediately, sprinkled with extra chopped herbs and handing some grated Parmesan cheese separately.

Easy-over Ravioli

TURKEY, TOMATO AND BASIL LASAGNE

Use finely chopped turkey breast, or, if preferred, chopped or minced chicken breast to make this tasty lasagne.

NUTRITION FACTS

Serves 4
Amount per serving 475g
Calories 533kcal/2255kJ

Total protein	38.4g
Total carbohydrate	74.6g
Sugars	10.7g
Total fat	11.1g
Saturated fat	2.8g
Polyunsaturated fat	0.8g
Monounsaturated fat	5g
Dietary fibre	5g
Sodium	306mg
Cholesterol	58mg

- ◆ 2 tbsp olive oil
- ◆ 1 large onion, peeled and finely chopped
- ◆ 2-3 garlic cloves, peeled and crushed
- ◆ 350 g/12 oz minced turkey
- ◆ 2 × 400 g/14 oz cans chopped tomatoes
- ◆ salt and ground black pepper

- ◆ 2 tbsp chopped fresh basil
- ◆ 6-8 fresh lasagne verdi sheets
- ◆ 225 g/8 oz courgettes, peeled, sliced lengthways and blanched
- ◆ 50 g/2 oz grated mozzarella cheese
- ◆ fresh basil sprigs

Preheat the oven to 190°C/375°F/Gas mark 5, 10 minutes before baking the lasagne. Heat the oil in a large pan and sauté the onion and garlic for 5 minutes or until the onion is softened. Add the minced turkey and continue to sauté for a further 5 minutes or until sealed.

Add the contents of the cans of tomatoes, bring to the boil, then reduce the heat and simmer for 10 minutes or until a thick consistency is formed. Season to taste and stir in the basil.

Bring a large pan of water to the boil, add 1 tablespoon salt, then drop in four lasagne sheets, one at a time. Cook for 2-3 minutes, ensuring that they do not stick together. Drain, lay them on clean teatowels and pat dry. Repeat with the remaining lasagne sheets.

Place about a third of the sauce in the base of an ovenproof dish and cover with a layer of blanched courgette slices, then 3-4 lasagne sheets. Repeat the layering, finishing with a layer of sauce. Sprinkle with the grated cheese. Bake the lasagne in the oven for 20-25 minutes or until the cheese is golden. Serve garnished with fresh basil sprigs.

RAVIOLI WITH MIXED MUSHROOMS

A good flavoured tomato sauce is an ideal choice to serve with this ravioli, with a final sprinkling of freshly grated Parmesan cheese to serve.

NUTRITION FACTS

Serves 4
Amount per serving 325g
Calories 509kcal/2137kJ

Total protein	19.2g
Total carbohydrate	63.7g
Sugars	5.5g
Total fat	21.7g
Saturated fat	10.2g
Polyunsaturated fat	1.9g
Monounsaturated fat	7.5g
Dietary fibre	3.9g
Sodium	450mg
Cholesterol	219mg

- ◆ 40 g/1½ oz butter
- ◆ 2 small onions, peeled and finely chopped
- ◆ 225 g/8 oz mixed mushrooms, finely chopped
- ◆ 100 g/4 oz ricotta cheese
- ◆ salt and ground black pepper

- ◆ batch basic pasta dough (see page 20)
- ◆ 300 ml/½ pt passata
- ◆ 2 tbsp chopped fresh basil
- ◆ freshly grated Parmesan cheese

For the filling, heat 1 ounce of butter in a small pan and gently sauté one onion for 5 minutes. Add the mushrooms and sauté for a further 5 minutes, stirring frequently. Remove from the heat and cool.

Beat the ricotta until smooth. Mix in the cooled mushrooms with seasoning to taste. Roll out the pasta dough and proceed to make the ravioli as shown on page 24.

For the sauce, melt the remaining butter in a pan and sauté the onion for 5 minutes. Add the passata and simmer for 10 minutes. Season to taste and add the basil.

Cook the ravioli in plenty of salted boiling water for 4-5 minutes or until "al dente" and drain. Return to the pan. Add the sauce and toss the cooked ravioli lightly until coated. Serve with the grated cheese.

Turkey, Tomato and Basil Lasagne

Salmon and Asparagus Ravioli

SALMON AND ASPARAGUS RAVIOLI

This recipe uses smoked salmon; however, it works very well with fresh salmon. If using fresh salmon, ensure that all the bones are removed before using.

- 4–5 asparagus spears, tough stems discarded
- 175 g/6 oz ricotta cheese
- 100 g/4 oz smoked salmon, cut into thin strips
- 2 tsp grated lemon zest
- ground black pepper
- batch basic pasta dough (see page 20)
- 150 ml/¼ pt soured cream
- 1 tbsp chopped fresh dill

Blanch the asparagus in boiling water for 2 minutes; drain. Blend the ricotta cheese and smoked salmon together in a bowl. Finely chop the blanched asparagus and stir into the smoked salmon mixture, together with the lemon zest and black pepper. Reserve.

Roll out the pasta dough and proceed to make the ravioli as previously described on page 24, placing the prepared filling in the hopper as before.

Cook the ravioli in salted boiling water for 4-5 minutes or until "al dente". Drain and return to the pan. Add the soured cream and dill. Heat through, gently stirring, for 2 minutes, then serve immediately.

NUTRITION FACTS

Serves 4
Amount per serving 261g
Calories 529kcal/2222kJ

Total protein	25.2g
Total carbohydrate	61.2g
Sugars	4g
Total fat	22.3g
Saturated fat	9.8g
Polyunsaturated fat	2.1g
Monounsaturated fat	8.2g
Dietary fibre	2.9g
Sodium	694mg
Cholesterol	232mg

PASTA ROULADE

This dish takes a little while to prepare but the finished result is well worth all the effort. You can vary the filling; try adding 50 g/2 oz chopped wild mushrooms or add some chopped prosciutto and peeled, seeded, chopped tomatoes.

- 25 g/1 oz butter
- 1 onion, peeled and chopped
- 2 garlic cloves, peeled and crushed
- 300 g/10 oz frozen chopped spinach, thawed
- 150 g/5 oz mushrooms, wiped and finely chopped
- 175 g/6 oz goat's cheese, crumbled
- 175 g/6 oz ricotta cheese
- salt and ground black pepper
- ½ tsp grated nutmeg
- 225 g/8 oz basic pasta dough (see page 20)
- 225 ml/8 fl oz vegetable stock
- 300 ml/½ pt Quick Tomato Sauce (see page 36)
- sprigs of basil

Preheat the oven to 190°C/375°F/Gas mark 5, 10 minutes before baking the pasta. For filling, melt the butter in a heavy pan and sauté the onion and garlic for 2 minutes. Squeeze out any excess moisture from the spinach. Add to the pan with the mushrooms and cook gently for 2 minutes. Stir in the goat cheese and ricotta with the seasoning to taste and nutmeg.

Using your pasta machine, roll out the pasta into 13 cm/5 in wide strips. Cut into 10 cm/4 in lengths. Cook the pasta sheets in plenty of salted boiling water, a few at a time, for 3-4 minutes. Stir occasionally to prevent the sheets sticking.

Remove the strips from the pan and drain thoroughly on clean teatowels.

Spread the pasta sheets with the filling and roll them up to encase it. Place in a buttered ovenproof dish. Pour the vegetable stock over the pasta, cover with aluminium foil and cook in the preheated oven for 20 minutes or until piping hot.

Meanwhile, reheat the prepared sauce. To serve, spoon a little of the prepared sauce onto each serving plate. Arrange 3-4 pasta rolls on top of the sauce. Garnish with the basil sprigs and serve immediately.

NUTRITION FACTS

Serves 4
Amount per serving 419g
Calories 478kcal/1999kJ

Total protein	20.9g
Total carbohydrate	38.5g
Sugars	8.3g
Total fat	28g
Saturated fat	12.9g
Polyunsaturated fat	2.2g
Monounsaturated fat	10.3g
Dietary fibre	4.5g
Sodium	1019mg
Cholesterol	125mg

CRAB AND SPRING ONION CANNELLONI

If you are fortunate enough to live in an area where freshly caught crabs are obtainable, this recipe is a must for you. However, it is possible to use canned or even frozen crab meat; just ensure that you gently squeeze out any excess moisture.

NUTRITION FACTS

Serves 4
Amount per serving 468g
Calories 692kcal/2929kJ

Total protein	36.9g
Total carbohydrate	110.9g
Sugars	11.9g
Total fat	14.3g
Saturated fat	3.6g
Polyunsaturated fat	1.7g
Monounsaturated fat	4.4g
Dietary fibre	6.4g
Sodium	572mg
Cholesterol	67mg

◆ 300 g/10 oz white crab meat
◆ 6 spring onions, trimmed and finely chopped
◆ 2-3 small jalapeño chillies, seeded and finely chopped
◆ 3 firm tomatoes, peeled, seeded and finely chopped
◆ salt and ground black pepper

◆ 10-12 fresh lasagne sheets
◆ 1 tbsp olive oil
◆ 1 medium onion, peeled and finely chopped
◆ 400 g/14 oz can chopped tomatoes
◆ 150 ml/¼ pt passata
◆ 50 g/2 oz grated Gruyère cheese
◆ sprigs of flat leaf parsley

Preheat the oven to 190°C/375°F/Gas mark 5, 10 minutes before baking the cannelloni. Place the crab meat, spring onions, chopped chillies and tomatoes with seasoning to taste in a bowl and mix together.

Bring a large pan of water to a boil, add 1 tablespoon salt, then drop in four lasagne sheets, one at a time. Cook for 2-3 minutes, ensuring that they do not stick together. Drain, lay them on clean teatowels and pat dry. Repeat with the remaining lasagne sheets.

Place about 2 tablespoons crab mixture at one end of a lasagne sheet. Moisten the edges and

roll up to encase the filling. Dampen the edge to seal. Place the filled tubes, seam side down, into the base of an ovenproof dish.

Heat the oil in a frying pan and sauté the onion for 5 minutes. Add the contents of the can of tomatoes and the passata and bring to the boil. Reduce the heat and simmer for 10 minutes. Season to taste.

Pour the sauce over the filled tubes and sprinkle with the cheese. Bake the cannelloni in the oven for 25 minutes or until golden. Garnish with fresh flat leaf parsley sprigs.

TORTELLONI WITH PRAWNS

When making stuffed pastas it is important to ensure that your pasta does not dry out while you are filling it. It is best to keep the dough you are not working with tightly covered in clingfilm.

NUTRITION FACTS

Serves 4
Amount per serving 323g
Calories 722kcal/3022kJ

Total protein	35g
Total carbohydrate	62.5g
Sugars	4.9g
Total fat	37.8g
Saturated fat	15.3g
Polyunsaturated fat	2.8g
Monounsaturated fat	16.5g
Dietary fibre	2.7g
Sodium	536mg
Cholesterol	358mg

◆ 50 g/2 oz freshly grated Parmesan cheese
◆ 100 g/4 oz peeled prawns
◆ 225 g/8 oz white fish fillets, skinned and boned
◆ 1 medium egg yolk
◆ 2 tbsp double cream
◆ salt and ground black pepper
◆ 1 tsp anchovy extract

◆ batch basic pasta dough (see page 20)
◆ 3 tbsp olive oil
◆ 4 shallots, peeled and finely chopped
◆ 1 tbsp tomato purée
◆ 4 tbsp dry white wine
◆ 150 ml/¼ pt soured cream
◆ 1 tbsp chopped fresh dill

For the filling, place the cheese, prawns, fish and egg yolk in a food processor. Blend, adding sufficient cream to form a thick filling. Season to taste and add the anchovy extract.

Roll out the pasta dough into 10 cm/3 in strips and use the prepared filling to make the tortelloni as previously described on page 83.

Cook the tortelloni in plenty of salted boiling

water for 4-5 minutes or until "al dente". Drain and return to the pan.

Meanwhile, for the sauce, heat the oil in a pan and sauté the shallots for 3 minutes. Blend the tomato purée with the wine and stir into the pan. Bring to the boil and simmer for 3 minutes.

Stir in the soured cream and dill, then heat for 1 minute. Pour over the pasta, toss and serve.

Crab and Spring Onion Cannelloni

BEEF AND MUSHROOM CANNELLONI

In this recipe I have used ceps and girolle mushrooms, but if you prefer,
you can use ordinary mushrooms.

NUTRITION FACTS

Serves 4
Amount per serving 407g
Calories 813kcal/3436kJ

Total protein	39.6g
Total carbohydrate	124.6g
Sugars	11.6g
Total fat	18g
Saturated fat	8.4g
Polyunsaturated fat	0.8g
Monounsaturated fat	4.7g
Dietary fibre	6.5g
Sodium	393mg
Cholesterol	59mg

- 225 ml/8 fl oz milk
- ½ small onion, peeled
- small piece carrot, peeled
- 1 celery stick, trimmed
- 2-3 whole cloves
- few black peppercorns
- 1-2 bayleaves
- few parsley stalks
- 25 g/1 oz butter or margarine
- 25 g/1 oz plain flour
- salt

- 15 g/½ oz dried ceps, soaked in warm water for 30 minutes
- 225 g/8 oz lean minced beef
- 1 onion, peeled and finely chopped
- 2 garlic cloves, peeled and crushed
- 75 g/3 oz girolle mushrooms, finely chopped
- 150 ml/¼ pt red wine
- 2 tbsp tomato purée
- ground black pepper
- 12 fresh lasagne sheets
- 75 g/3 oz sliced mozzarella cheese

Preheat the oven to 190°C/375°F/Gas mark 5, 10 minutes before baking the cannelloni. Pour the milk into a small saucepan and add the onion, carrot, celery, cloves, peppercorns, bayleaves and parsley stalks. Slowly bring the milk to just below boiling point then remove from the heat, cover and leave to infuse for at least 15 minutes. Strain, reserving the milk.

Melt the butter or margarine in a small pan and stir in the flour. Cook over a gentle heat for 2 minutes then draw off the heat and gradually stir in the reserved milk. Return pan to the heat and cook, stirring until smooth, thick and glossy. Season with the salt. Cover with a sheet of dampened greaseproof paper and reserve.

Drain the ceps, reserving the liquor and chop. Sauté the beef in a frying pan until browned, stirring to break up any lumps. Add the onion, garlic, ceps and girolles and continue to sauté for 5 minutes or until the onion is softened.

Pour in the wine, bring to the boil and simmer for 5 minutes. Blend the tomato purée with the reserved cep soaking water and 2 tablespoons of water. Stir into the beef mixture with black pepper to taste. Cook for another 5 minutes. Remove from the heat and cool.

Bring a large pan of water to the boil, add 1 tablespoon of salt, then drop in four lasagne sheets, one at a time. Cook for 2-3 minutes, ensuring that they do not stick together. Drain, lay them on clean dish towels and pat dry. Repeat with the remaining lasagne sheets.

Use the prepared beef mixture to fill the pasta sheets and roll up (see page 90). Place in the base of an ovenproof dish. Top with the prepared sauce and dot with the cheese slices. Bake the cannelloni in the oven for 25 minutes or until golden and bubbly. Serve immediately.

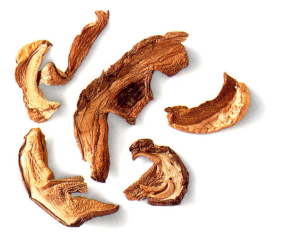

CHAPTER SEVEN

COLOURED AND FLAVOURED PASTAS

WITH THE WIDE ARRAY OF COLOURED, FLAVOURED PASTAS IT IS POSSIBLE TO MAKE, NO PASTA BOOK WOULD BE COMPLETE WITHOUT A COMPLETE CHAPTER DEVOTED TO THEM. FROM BLACK TO SAFFRON, RED TO GREEN, THERE IS ABSOLUTELY NO LIMIT TO THE COLOUR COMBINATIONS THAT CAN BE ACHIEVED, ESPECIALLY IF YOU TAKE INTO ACCOUNT THE SAUCES AND HERBS THAT CAN BE USED AS WELL.

TOMATO SPAGHETTI WITH MUSHROOMS

For this dish you need to include at least one kind of dried mushroom as this will give the depth of flavour that is so synonymous with all Italian mushroom-based dishes. Dried ceps keep so well, they are an ingredient that no well-stocked kitchen should be without.

NUTRITION FACTS

Serves 4
Amount per serving 275g
Calories 511kcal/2144kJ

Total protein	15.6g
Total carbohydrate	60.9g
Sugars	2.5g
Total fat	23.1g
Saturated fat	3.9g
Polyunsaturated fat	2.7g
Monounsaturated fat	14.4g
Dietary fibre	3.7g
Sodium	303mg
Cholesterol	178mg

For the sauce
◆ 15 g/½ oz dried ceps
◆ 3 tbsp olive oil
◆ 1 red onion, peeled and cut into wedges
◆ 3-6 smoked garlic cloves, peeled and thinly sliced
◆ 175 g/6 oz mushrooms, such as oyster or chanterelle, wiped and sliced
◆ 175 g/6 oz button mushrooms, wiped and sliced

◆ 6 tbsp red wine
◆ 2 tbsp extra virgin olive oil
◆ salt and ground black pepper
◆ 2 tbsp chopped fresh sage

To serve
◆ 450 g/1 lb fresh tomato spaghetti
◆ fresh chopped sage leaves

Soak the ceps in warm water for about 30 minutes. Drain, reserving the soaking liquid and chop the ceps.

Heat the oil in a pan and sauté the onion and garlic for 3 minutes. Add the chopped ceps, oyster or chanterelle and button mushrooms. Sauté for a further 5 minutes, stirring frequently.

Strain the cep soaking liquid into the pan and add the red wine. Bring to the boil, then simmer for 5 minutes or until the mushrooms are just cooked and the liquid has been reduced by about half. Stir in the extra virgin olive oil, seasoning to taste and sage. Cover with lid, remove from the heat and reserve.

Meanwhile, cook the tomato spaghetti in plenty of salted boiling water for 1-2 minutes or until "al dente." Drain and return to the pan. Add the mushrooms and sauce and toss

BEETROOT AND CHEESE RAVIOLI

I am a great fan of beetroot and cheese; the combination, to my mind, has no equal. Try this exciting combination and taste for yourself.

NUTRITION FACTS

Serves 4
Amount per serving 235g
Calories 514kcal/2163kJ

Total protein	24.1g
Total carbohydrate	62.2g
Sugars	5.1g
Total fat	20.7g
Saturated fat	8.9g
Polyunsaturated fat	1.8g
Monounsaturated fat	7.7g
Dietary fibre	2.3g
Sodium	436mg
Cholesterol	271mg

◆ 225 g/8 oz ricotta cheese
◆ 50 g/2 oz grated Gruyère cheese
◆ 2 tbsp snipped fresh chives
◆ 1 medium egg yolk

◆ salt and ground black pepper
◆ batch beetroot pasta dough
◆ 150 ml/¼ pt natural yogurt
◆ freshly snipped chives

Blend the ricotta, Gruyère cheese, chives, egg yolk and seasoning together in a bowl until smooth. Reserve.

Roll the pasta dough out and proceed to make the ravioli as previously described on page 24. Once one sheet of dough has been filled, repeat until all the dough and filling has been used. Let the ravioli dry on clean teatowels for 1 hour before cooking.

Cook the ravioli in plenty of salted boiling water for 4-5 minutes or until "al dente." Drain and return to the pan. Add the yogurt and stir lightly. Sprinkle with the snipped chives and serve immediately.

Tomato Spaghetti with Mushrooms

Black Tagliolini with Leeks and Orange

BLACK TAGLIOLINI WITH LEEKS AND ORANGE

Serve this colourful and attractive dish scattered with lashings of freshly shaved Pecorino Romano cheese, a tossed green salad and plenty of Italian crusty bread.

For the sauce
- 25 g/1 oz butter
- 225 g/8 oz small leeks, sliced
- 175 g/6 oz baby corn, halved
- grated zest and juice of 1 large orange
- 1 large orange, cut into sections
- 25 g/1 oz pecan halves, roughly chopped

- 4 tbsp dry white wine
- salt and ground black pepper

To serve
- 450 g/1 lb fresh black tagliolini
- freshly shaved Pecorino Romano cheese

Melt the butter in a pan and sauté the leeks for 3 minutes or until just beginning to soften. Add the corn, orange zest and juice and heat through for 2-3 minutes. Add the orange pieces with the chopped pecan halves, wine and seasoning to taste. Cover with a lid, remove from the heat and reserve.

Meanwhile, cook the black tagliolini in plenty of salted boiling water for 1-2 minutes or until "al dente". Drain and return to the pan. Add the leek and orange sauce, toss lightly, then serve sprinkled with the shaved cheese.

NUTRITION FACTS

Serves 4
Amount per serving 297g
Calories 505kcal/2122kJ

Total protein	17.9g
Total carbohydrate	64.6g
Sugars	6.7g
Total fat	20.3g
Saturated fat	6.7g
Polyunsaturated fat	2.8g
Monounsaturated fat	8.7g
Dietary fibre	5.2
Sodium	867mg
Cholesterol	198mg

LASAGNE VERDI WITH MUSHROOMS AND RAGU SAUCE

This is a dish that is ideal for freezing, so when you have plenty of time, make this, then freeze it ready for use at a later date. Use any mix of mushrooms you like. You can sprinkle the yogurt topping with some grated mozzarella cheese.

- 3 tbsp olive oil
- 350 g/12 oz mixed mushrooms, sliced
- Ragu Sauce (see page 38)

- 6-8 fresh lasagne verdi sheets
- 2 medium eggs
- 150 ml/¼ pt Greek-style yogurt

Preheat the oven to 190°C/375°F/Gas mark 5, 10 minutes before baking the lasagne. Heat the oil in a pan and gently sauté the mushrooms for 5 minutes, stirring occasionally, until softened. Remove from the heat and drain. Warm the Ragu Sauce if made previously and stir well.

Bring a large pan of water to the boil, add 1 tablespoon salt, then drop in four lasagne sheets, one at a time. Cook for 2-3 minutes, ensuring that they do not stick together. Drain and lay them on clean teatowels and pat dry. Repeat with the remaining lasagne sheets.

Place a layer of the Ragu Sauce in the base of an ovenproof dish and cover with 3-4 sheets of lasagne. Cover the lasagne with half the cooked mushrooms and top with the remaining Ragu Sauce. Cover with remaining lasagne sheets, then the rest of the mushrooms.

Beat the eggs with the yogurt and pour over the mushrooms. Cook the lasagne in the oven for 30 minutes or until golden.

NUTRITION FACTS

Serves 4
Amount per serving 572g
Calories 751kcal/3156kJ

Total protein	38.6g
Total carbohydrate	76.3g
Sugars	12.5g
Total fat	30.8g
Saturated fat	8.5g
Polyunsaturated fat	2.4g
Monounsaturated fat	15.8g
Dietary fibre	5.8g
Sodium	359mg
Cholesterol	173mg

WHOLEWHEAT SPAGHETTINI WITH AVOCADO

Most people never think of cooking with avocados; this is a shame as their creamy texture makes an ideal sauce when puréed. Their flesh also works well if used when still reasonably firm and added to pasta or stir fry at the end of the cooking time.

NUTRITION FACTS

Serves 4
Amount per serving 447g
Calories 656kcal/2748kJ

Total protein	21.4g
Total carbohydrate	68g
Sugars	9.6g
Total fat	33.7g
Saturated fat	8.3g
Polyunsaturated fat	3.9g
Monounsaturated fat	18.9g
Dietary fibre	7.1g
Sodium	753mg
Cholesterol	192mg

For the sauce
- 1 ripe avocado and 1 slightly firmer avocado
- 2 tbsp lemon juice
- 3 tbsp olive oil
- 4 plum tomatoes, peeled, seeded, and sliced
- 1 red pepper, seeded and sliced
- 1 yellow pepper, seeded and sliced
- 6 tbsp dry white wine
- 6 spring onions, trimmed and diagonally sliced
- 100 g/4 oz Parma ham, thinly sliced and cut into strips
- salt and ground black pepper
- 2 tbsp soured cream
- 2 tbsp chopped fresh basil

To serve
- 450 g/1 lb fresh wholewheat spaghettini

Peel the ripe avocado, discard the seed, then blend in a food processor with the lemon juice. Scrape into a small bowl and cover with plastic wrap. Peel, discard the seed from the other avocado and chop. Cover with clingfilm and reserve both avocados.

Heat the oil in a pan and sauté the sliced tomatoes and peppers for 5 minutes, stirring frequently. Add the white wine and simmer gently for 3 minutes.

Add the spring onions, the Parma ham, seasoning to taste and sliced avocado to the pan. Blend the puréed avocado with the soured cream and stir into the pan. Heat through for 2-3 minutes, then stir in the basil. Cover with a lid, remove the pan from the heat and keep warm while cooking the pasta.

Cook the spaghettini in plenty of salted boiling water for 1-2 minutes or until "al dente". Drain and return to the pan. Add the sauce to the pasta and toss lightly. Serve immediately.

Wholewheat Spaghettini with Avocado

SAFFRON FUSILLI WITH PEAS AND CHÈVRE

There are many different chèvres. Some are very salty and sharp while others are much milder and less salty. If you have not eaten chèvre before, choose one that is mild before you sample the sharper varieties.

NUTRITION FACTS

Serves 4
Amount per serving 302g
Calories 606kcal/2541kJ

Total protein	22.5g
Total carbohydrate	64.1g
Sugars	5.3g
Total fat	28.8g
Saturated fat	9.3g
Polyunsaturated fat	2.4g
Monounsaturated fat	14.4g
Dietary fibre	3.6g
Sodium	433mg
Cholesterol	178mg

For the sauce
◆ 4 tbsp olive oil
◆ 3-4 garlic cloves, peeled and sliced
◆ 1 large onion, peeled and sliced
◆ 120 ml/4 fl oz dry white wine
◆ 225 g/8 oz sugar snap peas, trimmed and halved

◆ 225 g/8 oz herb-crushed chèvre, diced

To serve
◆ 450 g/1 lb fresh saffron fusille
◆ fresh flat leaf parsley sprigs

Heat the oil in a pan and sauté the garlic and onion for 5 minutes. Add the white wine, bring to the boil and simmer for 3 minutes.

Blanch the sugar snap peas in a pan of boiling water for 1 minute. Drain and refresh in cold water. Add to the pan with the diced herb-crushed chèvre. Heat through very gently for 3 minutes, stirring occasionally.

Meanwhile, cook the saffron fusilli in plenty of salted boiling water for 1-2 minutes or until "al dente". Drain and return to the pan. Add the sugar snap peas and chèvre mixture. Toss lightly, garnish with the parsley and then serve.

MUSHROOM TAGLIATELLE WITH SAUSAGE AND TOMATO

This recipe is based on the traditional English breakfast which is rapidly disappearing due to changing lifestyles and eating habits. This recipe is however, far healthier and, in my opinion, tastier.

NUTRITION FACTS

Serves 4
Amount per serving 330g
Calories 715kcal/2991kJ

Total protein	25.3g
Total carbohydrate	67.8g
Sugars	5.7g
Total fat	40.3g
Saturated fat	11.9g
Polyunsaturated fat	4.4g
Monounsaturated fat	20.7g
Dietary fibre	3.8g
Sodium	797mg
Cholesterol	329mg

For the sauce
◆ 3 tbsp olive oil
◆ 1 onion, peeled and chopped
◆ 225 g/8 oz pork sausages, sliced
◆ 4 firm tomatoes, peeled, seeded and chopped
◆ 2 tbsp chopped fresh flat leaf parsley

◆ salt and ground black pepper
◆ 2 medium eggs

To serve
◆ 450 g/1 lb fresh mushroom tagliatelle
◆ freshly shaved Pecorino Romano cheese

Heat the oil in a frying pan and sauté the onion for 5 minutes or until softened. Add the sliced sausages and sauté for 2 more minutes. Stir in the tomatoes, cover with a lid and remove from the heat. Reserve.

Meanwhile cook the mushroom tagliatelle in plenty of salted boiling water for 1-2 minutes or until "al dente". Drain and return to the pan.

Add the sausage mixture, parsley and seasoning to taste and stir lightly. Heat through for 1 minute then remove from the heat. Beat the eggs and stir into the pasta, letting the heat of the pasta cook the eggs. Once the eggs have cooked, serve topped with fresh shavings of cheese.

Saffron Fusilli with Peas and Chèvre

Black Spaghettini with Sautéed Prawns

BLACK SPAGHETTINI WITH SAUTÉED PRAWNS

The colours of this dish are simply stunning and, for even greater effect, choose carefully the colour of the plate you serve it on.

For the sauce
- 3 tbsp olive oil
- 4 shallots, peeled and sliced into thin wedges
- 2-3 serrano or cayenne chillies, seeded and chopped
- 2-3 garlic cloves, peeled and thinly sliced
- 300 g/10 oz large prawns, shelled but tails left intact

- 100 g/4 oz sugar snap peas, trimmed
- 4 tbsp dry white wine
- grated zest of 1 lime
- 1 tbsp balsamic vinegar

To serve
- 450 g/1 lb fresh black spaghettini
- lime zest and lime slices to garnish

Heat the oil in a pan and sauté the shallots, chillies, and garlic for 3 minutes. Add the prawns and continue to sauté for 5 minutes or until the prawns have just begun to turn pink.

Cut the sugar snap peas into three and add to the pan with the wine and simmer for 2 minutes. Stir in the lime zest and balsamic vinegar. Cover with a lid, remove from the heat and keep warm while cooking the pasta.

Cook the black spaghettini pasta in plenty of salted boiling water for 1 minute or until "al dente". Drain and return to the pan. Add the cooked prawns and sauce, toss lightly, garnish and serve immediately.

NUTRITION FACTS

Serves 4
Amount per serving 278g
Calories 507kcal/2132kJ

Total protein	27.4g
Total carbohydrate	61.6g
Sugars	3.4g
Total fat	17.5g
Saturated fat	3.1g
Polyunsaturated fat	2g
Monounsaturated fat	10.5g
Dietary fibre	3.1g
Sodium	310mg
Cholesterol	325mg

TOMATO PAPPARDALLE WITH THREE CHEESES

Here I have combined three of Italy's great cheeses to provide a quick and creamy sauce with a subtle hint of lemon and parsley.

For the sauce
- 100 g/4 oz Gorgonzola cheese
- 200 ml/7 fl oz double cream
- 50 g/2 oz freshly grated Parmesan cheese
- 100 g/4 oz fontina cheese
- grated zest of 1 large lemon
- 2 tbsp chopped fresh flat leaf parsley
- 50 g/2 oz walnuts, roughly chopped

To serve
- 450 g/1 lb fresh tomato pappardalle
- sprigs of flat leaf parsley and lemon zest to garnish

Cut the Gorgonzola into small cubes and place in a saucepan with the double cream, Parmesan and fontina cheese. Heat gently, stirring until completely melted.

Stir in the lemon zest with the chopped parsley and walnuts. Cover with a lid, remove from the heat and keep warm.

Meanwhile, cook the tomato pappardalle in plenty of salted boiling water for 1-2 minutes or until "al dente". Drain and return to the pan. Add the cheese sauce, toss lightly, garnish and serve immediately.

NUTRITION FACTS

Serves 4
Amount per serving 251g
Calories 857kcal/3573kJ

Total protein	28.6g
Total carbohydrate	60.4g
Sugars	3.1g
Total fat	57.6g
Saturated fat	27.9g
Polyunsaturated fat	8.5g
Monounsaturated fat	16.9g
Dietary fibre	2.9g
Sodium	856mg
Cholesterol	278mg

PASTA ROSSA WITH ASPARAGUS AND SMOKED HAM

*Asparagus is delicious when lightly sautéed in a good oil and served "al dente".
Here the addition of the smoked ham gives this dish a slightly earthy flavour which
combines well with the flavoured pasta.*

NUTRITION FACTS

Serves 4
Amount per serving 333g
Calories 660kcal/2763kJ

Total protein	24.8g
Total carbohydrate	61.3g
Sugars	3.6g
Total fat	34.9g
Saturated fat	13.2g
Polyunsaturated fat	2.81g
Monounsaturated fat	15.9g
Dietary fibre	4g
Sodium	1183mg
Cholesterol	215mg

For the sauce
- 4 tbsp olive oil
- 6 shallots, peeled and sliced
- 2 garlic cloves, peeled and crushed
- 2 celery sticks, trimmed and chopped
- small bunch baby asparagus, trimmed and cut in half
- 120 ml/4 fl oz dry white wine

- 175 g/6 oz smoked ham, cut into strips
- 4 tbsp mascarpone
- salt and ground black pepper
- 2 tbsp chopped flat leaf parsley

To serve
- 450 g/1 lb fresh beetroot spaghetti
- sprigs of flat leaf parsley to garnish

Heat the oil in a pan and sauté the shallots, garlic and celery for 5 minutes or until softened. Add the asparagus and sauté for 1 more minute.

Add the wine, bring to the boil and simmer for 5 minutes or until the wine has been reduced by about half. Add the ham, cover with a lid and remove from the heat.

Meanwhile, cook the beetroot spaghetti in plenty of boiling salted water for 1-2 minutes or until "al dente". Drain and return to the pan. Add the asparagus mixture to the beetroot spaghetti pasta with the mascarpone, seasoning and parsley. Toss lightly until coated, garnish and serve immediately.

MIXED HERB SPAGHETTI WITH MASCARPONE AND SPINACH

*This creamy sauce is simple to make, delicious to eat and is an ideal meal to serve
when you wish to impress but time is short.*

NUTRITION FACTS

Serves 4
Amount per serving 321g
Calories 628kcal/2624kJ

Total protein	17.4g
Total carbohydrate	64.1g
Sugars	5.8g
Total fat	35.5g
Saturated fat	18.4g
Polyunsaturated fat	2.6g
Monounsaturated fat	11.7g
Dietary fibre	5.1g
Sodium	566mg
Cholesterol	234mg

For the sauce
- 25 g/1 oz butter
- 1 onion, peeled and chopped
- 2-3 smoked garlic cloves, peeled and thinly sliced
- 1 red pepper, seeded and chopped
- 2 tbsp roughly chopped fresh thyme
- 350 g/12 oz fresh spinach, cleaned and shredded

- 175 g/6 oz mascarpone cheese
- salt and ground black pepper
- ½-1 tsp grated nutmeg

To serve
- 450 g/1 lb fresh mixed herb spaghetti

Melt the butter in a pan and sauté the onion and garlic for 5 minutes. Add the pepper and continue to sauté for 3 minutes. Stir in the thyme and spinach, and heat through for 5 minutes. Stir in the mascarpone cheese, seasoning to taste and the nutmeg. Continue to

heat through gently for a further 3-5 minutes, until hot, stirring occasionally.

Meanwhile, cook the mixed herb spaghetti in plenty of salted boiling water for 1-2 minutes or until "al dente". Drain and return to the pan. Add the sauce, toss lightly and serve.

CHAPTER EIGHT

SALADS

HERE IS A GREAT SELECTION OF PASTA SALADS TO SERVE AS SNACKS, LUNCHES, EVEN MAIN MEALS. DIFFERENT TYPES OF PASTA ARE USED AND ARE COMBINED WITH AN EXCITING VARIETY OF INGREDIENTS AND FLAVOURFUL DRESSINGS. IT IS IMPORTANT TO BALANCE THE SHAPE AND COLOUR OF THE PASTA WITH THE OTHER INGREDIENTS TO MAKE THE SALAD AS ATTRACTIVE AS POSSIBLE.

PASTA AND WALDORF SALAD

This recipe is based on the famous Waldorf salad, of which every serious cook has their own interpretation. I would recommend that you try this salad as it gives an exciting new look to the original recipe.

NUTRITION FACTS

Serves 4
Amount per serving 314g
Calories 424kcal/1779kJ

Total protein	12.3g
Total carbohydrate	49g
Sugars	19.4g
Total fat	21.4g
Saturated fat	2.7g
Polyunsaturated fat	3.1g
Monounsaturated fat	8g
Dietary fibre	5g
Sodium	378mg
Cholesterol	99mg

For the salad

- 2 red apples, rinsed, cored and thinly sliced
- 2 ripe pears, rinsed, cored and sliced
- juice of 1 lemon
- 4 celery sticks, trimmed and sliced
- 50 g/2 oz pecan halves
- 225 g/8 oz fresh pasta, such as brandelle
- 1 small head Cos lettuce
- freshly shaved Pecorino Romano cheese

For the dressing

- 3 tbsp reduced calorie mayonnaise
- 2 tbsp fromage frais
- 1-2 tsp medium hot curry powder

Place the apples and pears in a bowl, pour over the lemon juice and toss lightly. Add the sliced celery and pecan halves, and mix lightly.

Cook the pasta in plenty of salted boiling water for 1-2 minutes or until "al dente". Drain and add to the celery.

Blend together the mayonnaise, fromage frais and curry powder to taste, reserve. Rinse the lettuce and use to line a salad bowl. Pile the prepared salad into the centre and drizzle over the dressing. Sprinkle with the freshly shaved Pecorino Romano cheese.

RAVIOLI SALAD

For this dish you do need good quality fresh flat leaf parsley, as the sprigs of parsley are encased in the pasta then cooked and tossed in a herb vinaigrette.

NUTRITION FACTS

Serves 4
Amount per serving 170g
Calories 450kcal/1877kJ

Total protein	17.4g
Total carbohydrate	30.3g
Sugars	1.2g
Total fat	30g
Saturated fat	5.1g
Polyunsaturated fat	2.7g
Monounsaturated fat	17.2g
Dietary fibre	1.5g
Sodium	660mg
Cholesterol	327mg

For the salad

- ½ batch basic pasta dough (see page 20)
- small bunch flat leaf parsley, rinsed
- 50 g/2 oz can anchovy fillets, drained (and soaked, optional)
- 2 tbsp capers (soaked if preferred)
- 4 hard boiled eggs, shelled and sliced

For the dressing

- 6 tbsp extra virgin olive oil
- 2 garlic cloves, peeled and crushed
- 2 shallots, peeled and finely chopped
- 1 tbsp chopped fresh flat leaf parsley
- 1 tbsp chopped fresh basil
- salt and ground black pepper
- 1 tbsp balsamic vinegar

Using your pasta machine, roll out the pasta dough to form strips about 13 cm/5 in wide. Place sprigs of the flat leaf parsley on half the dough, dampen edges and fold over the other half of the pasta.

Using a fluted cutter, cut out squares ensuring that each square contains a sprig of parsley. Sprinkle with a little flour and let dry for about 1 hour.

For the salad dressing, heat the oil in a pan, and gently fry the garlic and shallots for 5 minutes or until softened. Remove the pan from the heat and stir in the herbs, seasoning and vinegar. Cover and reserve.

Cook the ravioli squares in plenty of salted boiling water until "al dente". Drain and return to the pan. Pour over the prepared dressing and toss lightly. Arrange the ravioli in a warmed serving bowl. Top with the anchovy fillets, capers and sliced hard boiled eggs, then serve.

Pasta and Waldorf Salad

FARFALLE WITH MARINATED PEPPERS

Skinning the peppers before marinating ensures that the peppers absorb the marinade flavour quicker. The peppers are far easier to digest once skinned and the flesh is sweeter too.

NUTRITION FACTS

Serves 4
Amount per serving 352g
Calories 450kcal/1887kJ

Total protein	12.6g
Total carbohydrate	50.3g
Sugars	11.7
Total fat	23.6g
Saturated fat	4.6g
Polyunsaturated fat	2.5g
Monounsaturated fat	14.8g
Dietary fibre	5.3g
Sodium	250mg
Cholesterol	94mg

For the salad
◆ 2 red peppers, seeded
◆ 2 yellow peppers, seeded
◆ 2 green peppers, seeded
◆ 6 tbsp olive oil
◆ 1-2 garlic cloves, peeled and crushed
◆ 1 jalapeño chilli, seeded and finely chopped
◆ 2 tbsp lemon juice
◆ grated zest of ½ lemon
◆ 1 tbsp chopped fresh basil
◆ 2 slices thick white bread

To serve
◆ salad leaves
◆ 225 g/8 oz fresh pasta, such as farfalle
◆ freshly shaved Parmesan cheese
◆ extra grated lemon zest

Preheat grill to high and line the grill rack with foil, or use a barbecue. Cut the peppers into quarters and place skin side up on the grill rack. Grill for 10 minutes or until skins have blistered and blackened. Remove from the heat and place in a plastic bag and leave until cool.

Once cool, skin the peppers and slice thinly. Place the peppers in a shallow dish and pour over the oil. Sprinkle with the crushed garlic, chilli, lemon juice and zest and basil. Cover and leave in the refrigerator for at least 2 hours, turning occasionally.

Cut the bread into cubes. Drain the peppers and reserve both peppers and marinade. Heat 3 tablespoons of the marinade in a frying pan and fry the bread cubes, stirring frequently. Drain on absorbent kitchen paper; reserve.

Cook the pasta in plenty of salted boiling water for 1-2 minutes or until "al dente". Drain and return to the pan. Mix the marinated peppers with the cooked pasta.

Arrange the salad leaves in a serving bowl. Pile the pepper and pasta mix on top of the salad greens. Pour over the marinade and scatter over the croûtons. Serve with freshly shaved Parmesan cheese and grated lemon zest.

Farfalle with Marinated Peppers

Minty Crab, Pear and Pasta Salad

MINTY CRAB, PEAR AND PASTA SALAD

I found the dressing used in this recipe while looking through an old cookbook. I have updated it by using a flavoured vinegar and oil, and I am sure that once you have tried this recipe it will quickly become a firm favourite.

For the salad
◆ 225 g/8 oz cooked fresh pasta, such as tricoloured spaghetti
◆ 200 g/7 oz white crab meat, flaked
◆ 2 oranges, peeled and cut into sections
◆ 2 pink grapefruit, peeled and cut into sections
◆ 2 tbsp chopped fresh mint
◆ 50 g/2 oz pecan halves

For the dressing
◆ 2 ripe pears
◆ 120 ml/4 fl oz walnut oil
◆ 4 tbsp extra virgin olive oil
◆ 1 tbsp orange or raspberry vinegar
◆ salt and ground black pepper

Place the cooked pasta in a bowl and add the flaked crab meat, orange and grapefruit sections, chopped mint and pecan halves. Toss lightly and spoon into a serving bowl.

For the dressing, peel and core the pears, then place in a food processor. Gradually blend the pears with the walnut oil and then the olive oil. Add the vinegar with seasoning and blend for 30 seconds or until smooth. Pour over the salad, toss lightly and serve.

NUTRITION FACTS

Serves 4
Amount per serving 494g
Calories 674kcal/2799kJ

Total protein	14.9g
Total carbohydrate	35.9g
Sugars	23.5g
Total fat	53.2g
Saturated fat	5.4g
Polyunsaturated fat	25.2g
Monounsaturated fat	19.1g
Dietary fibre	5.9g
Sodium	318mg
Cholesterol	36mg

PASTA AND YOGURT SALAD

There are many different ingredients that can be used as salad dressings. Yogurt makes an ideal base for a salad dressing, and with more people watching their intake of fat, yogurt is an obvious choice.

For the salad
◆ 2 oranges
◆ 1 tbsp olive oil
◆ 225 g/8 oz leeks, sliced
◆ 2 tbsp pine nuts
◆ 2 tbsp roughly chopped fresh flat leaf parsley
◆ 100 g/4 oz broccoli florets
◆ 100 g/4 oz young carrots, chopped

◆ 100 g/4 oz mortadella, sliced into strips
◆ 150 ml/¼ pt low-fat natural yogurt
◆ salt and ground black pepper
◆ radicchio leaves

To serve
◆ 225 g/8 oz fresh pasta, such as tricoloured farfalle

Remove the zest from one of the oranges, then peel and divide both oranges into sections. Reserve zest and orange sections.

Heat the oil in a frying pan and sauté the leeks for 5 minutes or until just softened. Add the orange zest and pine nuts, and continue to sauté for 2 minutes. Remove from the heat, stir in the parsley and place in a bowl.

Divide the broccoli into smaller florets and blanch in lightly salted boiling water for 2 minutes. Drain and plunge into cold water. Drain again, and add to the leeks.

Cook the carrots in lightly salted boiling water for 5 minutes or until just cooked. Drain and add to the vegetables.

Cook the pasta in plenty of salted boiling water for 1-2 minutes or until "al dente". Drain and return to the pan.

Add the mortadella to the pasta with the vegetables and orange sections. Stir in the yogurt with seasoning to taste. Mix lightly together. Line a serving bowl with the radicchio leaves. Spoon the salad into the bowl and serve.

NUTRITION FACTS

Serves 4
Amount per serving 335g
Calories 392kcal/1646kJ

Total protein	15.8g
Total carbohydrate	43.9g
Sugars	14.4g
Total fat	18.4g
Saturated fat	4.1g
Polyunsaturated fat	4.4g
Monounsaturated fat	8.3g
Dietary fibre	5.7g
Sodium	499mg
Cholesterol	105mg

FARFALLE AND MIXED VEGETABLE MEDLEY

When cooking pasta, you may find that sometimes you have leftover pasta.
This is ideal to use as the basis of a delicious salad. The short pastas and shapes
are better suited.

NUTRITION FACTS

Serves 4
Amount per serving 250g
Calories 213kcal/891kJ

Total protein	5.3g
Total carbohydrate	23.5g
Sugars	5.4g
Total fat	11.5g
Saturated fat	2.5g
Polyunsaturated fat	2.7g
Monounsaturated fat	6.1g
Dietary fibre	2.4g
Sodium	575mg
Cholesterol	8mg

For the salad
- 100 g/4 oz sugar snap peas
- 6 spring onions, trimmed
- 1 small bunch radishes, trimmed
- 75 g/3 oz baby corn
- 100 g/4 oz cherry tomatoes
- 50 g/2 oz rocket, rinsed
- 300 g/10 oz cooked fresh farfalle

For the dressing
- 5 tbsp reduced calorie mayonnaise
- 3 tbsp lemon juice
- 2 tbsp chopped fresh basil

Cut the sugar snap peas in half, then blanch in lightly salted boiling water for 1 minute. Drain and plunge into cold water, drain again and place in a serving bowl.

Slice the spring onions diagonally and add to the peas. Cut about 4-5 radishes into roses if liked and leave in cold water to open. Slice the remaining radishes and add to the bowl. Cut the baby corn and tomatoes in half; add to the bowl with the rocket and cooked farfalle. Toss ingredients lightly together.

Place the dressing ingredients in a screw top jar and shake vigorously. Pour over the salad, toss lightly and serve garnished with the radish roses.

CORONATION TURKEY PASTA

This makes a delicious, filling salad. Ideal for entertaining or for when a more substantial meal is required.

For the dressing
- 2 tbsp olive oil
- 1 small onion
- 1 tbsp medium hot curry powder
- 150 ml/¼ pt dry white wine
- 50 g/2 oz ready-to-eat dried apricots, chopped
- 4 tbsp reduced calorie mayonnaise
- 2 tbsp soured cream

For the salad
- 225 g/8 oz cooked turkey meat, diced
- 300 g/10 oz cooked fresh pasta, such as brandelle
- 25 g/1 oz sliced toasted almonds
- salad leaves
- fresh apricot slices

For the salad dressing, heat the olive oil in a pan and gently sauté the onion for 5 minutes or until softened. Add the medium hot curry powder and sauté for 2 minutes, stirring frequently. Pour in the dry white wine with 3 tablespoons of water, add the chopped apricots and simmer gently for 10 minutes or until the apricots are soft and pulpy.

Remove from the heat and blend in a food processor to form a smooth purée. Mix the mayonnaise, soured cream and apricot purée together. Stir the diced turkey meat, cooked pasta and almonds into the dressing.

Arrange the salad leaves in the base of a serving platter, then pile the pasta mixture on top. Garnish with the apricot slices and serve.

NUTRITION FACTS

Serves 4
Amount per serving 258g
Calories 407kcal/1703kJ

Total protein	24.5g
Total carbohydrate	24.9g
Sugars	8.1g
Total fat	21.4g
Saturated fat	4.6g
Polyunsaturated fat	6.4g
Monounsaturated fat	9.2g
Dietary fibre	2.7g
Sodium	184mg
Cholesterol	63mg

PASTA NIÇOISE WITH BALSAMIC DRESSING

Since discovering balsamic vinegar, my salads have reached new heights in gastronomic experience. I would urge anyone who has not tried this vinegar to do so immediately.

For the salad
- 175 g/6 oz French green beans, trimmed
- 200 g/7 oz can tuna, drained
- 300 g/10 oz cooked fresh pasta, such as fusilli
- 2 tbsp chopped fresh flat leaf parsley
- 2 large tomatoes, sliced
- 2 medium hard boiled eggs, shelled and sliced
- 50 g/2 oz can anchovy fillets, drained (soaked if preferred)
- 50 g/2 oz black olives, stoned

For the dressing
- 5 tbsp extra virgin olive oil
- 1 tsp clear honey
- 1 tsp wholegrain mustard
- salt and ground black pepper
- 2 tbsp balsamic vinegar

Cook the French green beans in a pan of lightly salted boiling water for 4-5 minutes or until just cooked. Drain and plunge into cold water. Drain again and reserve. Divide the drained tuna into small chunks.

Mix the pasta and chopped parsley together and place in the base of a shallow serving platter

or dish. Arrange the cooked beans, sliced tomatoes, tuna, eggs, drained anchovies and olives attractively on top of the pasta.

Place the dressing ingredients in a screw top jar and shake vigorously. Pour over the salad just before serving.

NUTRITION FACTS

Serves 4
Amount per serving 301g
Calories 377kcal/1577kJ

Total protein	22.8g
Total carbohydrate	22.9g
Sugars	6.3g
Total fat	22.2g
Saturated fat	3.3g
Polyunsaturated fat	2.2g
Monounsaturated fat	12.5g
Dietary fibre	2.8g
Sodium	1099mg
Cholesterol	144mg

MELON, SMOKED CHICKEN AND PASTA SALAD

Use a selection of melons in this refreshing salad. The different colours of the melons make this an attractive dish.

NUTRITION FACTS

Serves 4
Amount per serving 304g
Calories 337kcal/1406kJ

Total protein	19.9g
Total carbohydrate	22.3g
Sugars	10.1g
Total fat	19.1g
Saturated fat	7g
Polyunsaturated fat	1.5g
Monounsaturated fat	9.4g
Dietary fibre	2.5g
Sodium	164mg
Cholesterol	61mg

For the salad
- 350 g/12 oz assorted melon slices
- 175 g/6 oz smoked chicken meat
- 225 g/8 oz cooked fresh mushroom pasta
- 1 large orange, peeled and segmented
- fresh spinach leaves
- 2 tbsp grated Gruyère cheese
- orange zest to garnish

For the dressing
- 4 tbsp soured cream
- 1 tsp wholegrain mustard
- 3 tbsp extra virgin olive oil
- 2 tbsp champagne or white wine vinegar

Discard the seeds and skin from the melons and cut into small dice. Place in a bowl.

Cut the smoked chicken into strips and add to the melon with the pasta and orange segments; mix lightly. Arrange the fresh spinach leaves on a serving platter.

For the dressing, place the soured cream in a bowl and beat in the mustard. Gradually beat in the olive oil, then the vinegar. Spoon the pasta onto the spinach lined platter, sprinkle with the grated cheese, garnish and serve. Hand the dressing separately.

SMOKED SALMON, PASTA AND RASPBERRY SALAD

I personally love the combination of sweet and savoury, especially if the sweet food is fruit. Here, sweet ripe raspberries are used with smoked salmon to give an interesting and stunning taste sensation.

NUTRITION FACTS

Serves 4
Amount per serving 188g
Calories 292kcal/1217kJ

Total protein	12.2g
Total carbohydrate	15.4g
Sugars	3.1g
Total fat	20.4g
Saturated fat	6.5g
Polyunsaturated fat	3.4g
Monounsaturated fat	9.3g
Dietary fibre	1.6g
Sodium	542mg
Cholesterol	32mg

For the dressing
- 4 tbsp raspberry vinegar
- 3 tbsp extra virgin olive oil
- 1 tbsp walnut oil
- pinch of mustard powder
- 4 tbsp soured cream

For the salad
- 225 g/8 oz fresh pasta, such as mixed herb fusilli
- 6 spring onions, trimmed
- 100 g/4 oz smoked salmon
- 100 g/4 oz fresh raspberries
- 50 g/2 oz watercress sprigs, rinsed
- freshly shaved Pecorino Romano cheese

For the dressing, blend the vinegar with the oils and mustard powder until thoroughly mixed, then stir in the soured cream. Cover and leave in the refrigerator for 30 minutes.

Cook the pasta in plenty of salted boiling water for 1-2 minutes or until "al dente". Drain and return to the pan.

Meanwhile, diagonally slice the spring onions, cut the smoked salmon into strips and pick over the fresh raspberries. Add the spring onions, smoked salmon, raspberries and watercress sprigs to the cooked pasta. Add the salad dressing and toss lightly. Serve, sprinkled with the freshly shaved cheese.

Melon, Smoked Chicken and Pasta Salad

FIG, PASTA AND PROSCIUTTO SALAD

Make the most of fresh figs when they are available. Whether it is the green or purple variety, their soft flesh, delicate flavour and attractive appearance make them an ideal salad ingredient.

NUTRITION FACTS

Serves 4
Amount per serving 314g
Calories 267kcal/1120kJ

Total protein	8.7g
Total carbohydrate	29.1g
Sugars	16.9g
Total fat	13.7g
Saturated fat	2.4g
Polyunsaturated fat	1.4g
Monounsaturated fat	9g
Dietary fibre	3.8g
Sodium	588mg
Cholesterol	5mg

For the salad
- 7.5 cm/3 in piece cucumber
- salt
- 100 g/4 oz prosciutto, sliced
- 2 ripe pears
- 1 tbsp orange juice
- 100 g/4 oz rocket
- 225 g/8 oz cooked fresh pasta, such as fusilli
- 4 fresh ripe figs

- edible flowers such as pansies, nasturtians, and primroses (optional)

For the dressing
- 3 tbsp orange juice
- 4 tbsp extra virgin olive oil
- 1 tsp clear honey
- 1-2 tsp Dijon-style mustard
- ground black pepper

Peel the cucumber and slice thinly. Sprinkle with salt and leave for 30 minutes. Rinse well in cold water and pat dry with absorbent kitchen paper. Place in a bowl with the prosciutto.

Rinse the ripe pears and peel if preferred. Core and slice thinly. Sprinkle with the fresh orange juice and add to the bowl. Tear the rocket into small pieces if the leaves are large and add to the bowl with the cooked pasta. Toss lightly together until mixed.

Slice the figs and add to the bowl. Spoon onto a serving platter.

Place the dressing ingredients into a screw top jar and shake vigorously until well blended. Pour over the pasta. Garnish the salad with the edible flowers and serve.

PASTA WITH TOMATO TAPENADE

Tapenade can be found throughout the Mediterranean and is delicious spread on toast as a tasty snack. It also can form the basis of an interesting salad, as this recipe illustrates.

NUTRITION FACTS

Serves 4
Amount per serving 220g
Calories 679kcal/2818kJ

Total protein	11.7g
Total carbohydrate	35.5g
Sugars	1.8g
Total fat	55.6g
Saturated fat	8g
Polyunsaturated fat	7g
Monounsaturated fat	34.2g
Dietary fibre	3.4g
Sodium	2006mg
Cholesterol	89mg

For the tapenade
- 225 g/8 oz black olives, stoned
- 6 sun-dried tomatoes
- 40 g/1½ oz capers (soaked if preferred)
- 1 tbsp chopped fresh parsley
- 2 garlic cloves, peeled and crushed
- 1 tsp wholegrain mustard
- 50 g/2 oz can anchovy fillets (soaked if preferred)
- 150 ml/¼ pt extra virgin olive oil
- ground black pepper

To serve
- 225 g/8 oz fresh pasta, such as mixed herb farfalle
- Cos lettuce
- sprigs of watercress
- 2 tbsp freshly made croûtons
- 50 g/2 oz halved cherry tomatoes

For the tomato tapenade, blend the black olives, sun-dried tomatoes, capers, chopped fresh parsley, garlic, wholegrain mustard and anchovies with their oil to a thick paste in a food processor. With the motor still running, gradually pour in the olive oil in a thin steady stream to form a thick purée. Add black pepper to taste and reserve.

Cook the pasta in plenty of salted boiling water for 1-2 minutes or until "al dente". Drain and return to the pan.

Meanwhile, rinse the lettuce and watercress leaves and use to line a salad bowl. Add the tapenade to the pasta and toss lightly. Serve in the lettuce-lined bowl, sprinkled with the croûtons. Garnish with the cherry tomatoes.

Fig, Pasta and Prosciutto Salad

Wild Mushroom and Pasta Salad

WILD MUSHROOM AND PASTA SALAD

For a more substantial salad, add some peeled prawns or a mixture of seafood.

For the salad
- 120 ml/4 fl oz virgin olive oil
- 4 shallots, peeled and sliced
- 2-3 garlic cloves, peeled and sliced
- 1-2 serrano chillies, seeded and sliced
- 4 sun-dried tomatoes, chopped
- 300 g/10 oz assorted wild mushrooms, such as oyster, girolle, chanterelle, wiped and sliced
- 4 tbsp dry white wine

- salt and ground black pepper
- 1-2 tsp truffle oil
- assorted bitter salad leaves, such as rocket, spinach, watercress or sorrel

To serve
- 225 g/8 oz fresh rigatoni
- few shavings black truffle (optional)
- sprigs flat leaf parsley to garnish

Heat the oil in a frying pan and sauté the shallots, garlic and chillies for 2 minutes. Add the sun-dried tomatoes and mushrooms; continue to sauté for 3 more minutes. Add the white wine and seasoning; simmer for 3-4 minutes or until the mushrooms are just tender.

Cook the pasta in plenty of salted boiling water for 1-2 minutes or until "al dente". Drain and return to the pan. Add the truffle oil to the pasta and heat through for 1 minute, stirring lightly. Stir in the sautéed mushroom mixture.

Line a salad bowl with the salad leaves and spoon the pasta salad on top. Sprinkle with the freshly shaved truffle, if used, garnish and serve.

NUTRITION FACTS

Serves 4
Amount per serving 225g
Calories 500kcal/2078kJ

Total protein	8.4g
Total carbohydrate	31.7g
Sugars	2.2g
Total fat	37.7g
Saturated fat	5.6g
Polyunsaturated fat	4.8g
Monounsaturated fat	25g
Dietary fibre	1.7g
Sodium	202mg
Cholesterol	89mg

PASTA AND DUCK SALAD

This flavourful salad is ideal for using up leftover roast duck. If you prefer, you can pan-fry duck breasts, drain thoroughly, then slice.

- 225 g/8 oz fresh farfalle
- 4 tbsp virgin olive oil
- 100 g/4 oz pancetta or smoked bacon, rinded and cut into strips
- 3 tbsp dry white wine
- 1 tbsp white wine vinegar
- salt and ground black pepper

- 225 g/8 oz roast duck, cut into strips
- 75 g/3 oz Gruyère cheese, diced
- 1 large orange, peeled and cut into sections
- roughly chopped fresh flat leaf parsley
- salad greens
- halved kumquats (optional) to garnish

Cook the farfalle in salted boiling water for 1-2 minutes or until "al dente". Drain and place in a bowl. Pour over the olive oil and toss lightly.

Meanwhile, place the pancetta or bacon in a non-stick frying pan and cook gently until crisp. Add the white wine and vinegar and simmer for 2 minutes, stirring occasionally.

Add the pancetta and liquid to the pasta with seasoning to taste, the duck strips, Gruyère cheese, orange sections and chopped parsley. Toss lightly.

Arrange the salad greens on a platter and spoon on the pasta mixture. Garnish with the kumquat halves and serve.

NUTRITION FACTS

Serves 4
Amount per serving 240g
Calories 520kcal/2172kJ

Total protein	31.3g
Total carbohydrate	32.8g
Sugars	4.3g
Total fat	29.4g
Saturated fat	9g
Polyunsaturated fat	2.7g
Monounsaturated fat	15.7g
Dietary fibre	2g
Sodium	830mg
Cholesterol	177mg

WARM AVOCADO, PARMA HAM AND PASTA SALAD

One of the joys of eating is the wide range of ingredients from all over the world which are so readily available to so many of us. This recipe includes ingredients that have been produced continents apart and yet the flavours balance harmoniously.

NUTRITION FACTS

Serves 4
Amount per serving 235g
Calories 594kcal/2471kJ

Total protein	14.8g
Total carbohydrate	36.1g
Sugars	5.3g
Total fat	44.6g
Saturated fat	7.3g
Polyunsaturated fat	6.9g
Monounsaturated fat	27.7
Dietary fibre	4.9g
Sodium	654mg
Cholesterol	93mg

For the salad
- 2 ripe but firm avocados
- 3 tbsp lime juice
- 4 tbsp extra virgin olive oil
- 1 red onion, peeled and cut into thin wedges
- 75 g/3 oz pecan halves
- 1 tbsp maple syrup

- 100 g/4 oz Parma ham, snipped into strips
- salt and ground black pepper
- red and green chicory leaves

To serve
- 225 g/8 oz fresh pasta, such as brandelle
- sprigs of flat leaf parsley

Peel, seed and dice the avocado. Place in a bowl and sprinkle with the lime juice, reserve.

Heat the oil in a frying pan and sauté the onion briskly until the edges are slightly blackened. Reduce the heat, add the pecans, and sauté for 1 minute. Remove from the heat and add the avocado with the lime juice, maple syrup, and Parma ham, and heat through for 2 minutes.

Cook the pasta in plenty of salted boiling water for 1-2 minutes or until "al dente". Drain and return to the pan. Pour over the avocado and ham mixture; add seasoning to taste. Heat through for 2 minutes, stirring lightly.

Meanwhile, line a serving platter with the red and green chicory leaves and pile the pasta mixture on top. Garnish with the parsley sprigs.

PARSLEY AND LEMON PASTA

This salad is quick, simple to prepare, and delicious to eat. It makes a refreshing change when you are searching for a new taste experience.

NUTRITION FACTS

Serves 4
Amount per serving 173g
Calories 402kcal/1680kJ

Total protein	13.9g
Total carbohydrate	33.7g
Sugars	4.9g
Total fat	24.6g
Saturated fat	5.7g
Polyunsaturated fat	4.2g
Monounsaturated fat	10.7g
Dietary fibre	1.7g
Sodium	791mg
Cholesterol	98mg

For the dressing
- 2 tbsp chopped fresh flat leaf parsley
- 1 tbsp chopped fresh mint
- grated zest of 1 lemon
- 2 garlic cloves, peeled and crushed
- 3 tbsp extra virgin olive oil
- 6 tbsp Greek-style yogurt
- 2-3 tbsp toasted pine nuts
- salt and ground black pepper

For the salad
- 225 g/8 oz fresh pasta, such as mushroom fusilli
- 50 g/2 oz baby spinach leaves, rinsed
- 2 tbsp capers (soaked if preferred)
- 50 g/2 oz can anchovy fillets, drained (soaked if preferred)

Blend the parsley, mint, lemon zest, garlic and oil together in a food processor to form a thick paste. With the motor still running, gradually blend in the yogurt to form a thick mayonnaise-style dressing. Scrape the yogurt mixture into a bowl and stir in the pine nuts with seasoning to taste. Reserve.

Meanwhile, cook the pasta in plenty of boiling salted water for 1-2 minutes or until "al dente". Drain and return to the pan. Add the dressing and stir until lightly coated.

Arrange the spinach leaves in a bowl and spoon the pasta on top. Sprinkle with the capers, arrange the anchovies on top, then serve.

CHAPTER NINE

DESSERTS

ALTHOUGH PASTA IS MAINLY A SAVOURY INGREDIENT, IT IS OFTEN USED IN DESSERTS. HERE, I HAVE COMBINED THE PASTA WITH VARIOUS INGREDIENTS TO CREATE SOME STUNNING AND UNUSUAL SWEET RECIPES; FROM SWEET FETTUCCINE WITH MAPLE SYRUP TO ORANGES WITH CHOCOLATE RIBBONS. IF YOU PLAN TO INDULGE IN A PASTA DESSERT, YOU SHOULD SERVE A LIGHTER MAIN COURSE.

ORANGES WITH CHOCOLATE RIBBONS

I have to admit to a passion for chocolate. Here I have combined it with oranges that have been marinated in brandy, providing a simple yet exotic dessert, suitable for any dinner party or special occasion.

- 4 large oranges
- 50 g/2 oz sugar
- 2-3 tbsp brandy
- 2-3 whole cloves
- 225 g/8 oz chocolate fettuccine

- 1 tbsp toasted flaked almonds
- 1 tbsp icing sugar, sifted
- lightly whipped double cream or Greek-style yogurt

Peel the oranges, taking care to remove all the bitter white pith. Slice thinly and place in a glass mixing bowl.

Dissolve the sugar with 150 ml/$^1/_4$ pt water in a heavy pan over moderate heat. Once dissolved, bring to the boil and boil for 5 minutes or until a light sugar syrup is formed.

Remove from the heat and stir in the brandy and cloves. Pour over the oranges. Leave for at least 2 hours, turning the oranges occasionally in the marinade.

Cook the chocolate fettuccine in plenty of boiling water for 1-2 minutes or until "al dente", then drain. Arrange on four individual serving plates. Spoon the oranges over the pasta and sprinkle with the toasted flaked almonds. Toss lightly and sprinkle with icing sugar. Serve with the cream or yogurt.

CHOCOLATE SPIRALS WITH PISTACHIO AND ROSE CREAM

Stirred into freshly whipped cream, rose water gives a lightly perfumed and fragrant cream which combines well with the raspberries and chocolate in this recipe.

For the dessert
- 25 g/1 oz unsalted shelled pistachio nuts
- 150 ml/$^1/_4$ pt double cream
- 1 tbsp rose water
- 300 g/10 oz fresh raspberries
- 225 g/8 oz fresh chocolate tagliatelle

To decorate
- rose petals

Preheat the oven to 200°C/400°F/Gas mark 6 and roast the pistachio nuts for 10 minutes. Remove from the oven, cool and roughly chop.

Whip the cream lightly, stir in the rose water and chill until required. Clean the raspberries, rinsing lightly and dry on paper towels.

Cook the chocolate tagliatelle in plenty of boiling water for 1-2 minutes or until "al dente". Drain and stir in the cream. Arrange the pasta in small nests with the raspberries. Scatter with the chopped pistachios and decorate with rose petals. Serve immediately.

Oranges with Chocolate Ribbons

Sweet Fettuccine with Maple Syrup

SWEET FETTUCCINE WITH MAPLE SYRUP

When using pasta for desserts, cook the pasta in unsalted water, then toss the cooked pasta in melted butter. Here I have used some toasted nuts to serve with the pasta and poured over maple syrup—certainly not for serious weight watchers!

For the dessert
- 100 g/4 oz mixed shelled nuts, such as pecan halves, skinned hazelnuts and blanched almonds
- 50 g/2 oz unsalted butter, melted
- 1 tsp ground cinnamon
- 4 tbsp maple syrup
- 225 g/8 oz fresh fettuccine

To decorate
- fresh strawberries
- sprigs of mint

Preheat the oven to 200°C/400°F/Gas mark 6 and roast the nuts for 10 minutes or until golden. Remove from the oven and cool.

Melt the unsalted butter in a pan and stir in the ground cinnamon, maple syrup and roasted mixed nuts.

Meanwhile, cook the fettuccine in plenty of boiling water for 1-2 minutes or until "al dente". Drain and return to the pan. Pour over the maple syrup and nut sauce and toss lightly. Serve immediately decorated with the strawberries, cut into fans and mint sprigs.

NUTRITION FACTS

Serves 4
Amount per serving 139g
Calories 472kcal/1967kJ

Total protein	10.3g
Total carbohydrate	42.3g
Sugars	12.2g
Total fat	30.2g
Saturated fat	9g
Polyunsaturated fat	4.2g
Monounsaturated fat	15.1g
Dietary fibre	3g
Sodium	180mg
Cholesterol	117mg

FARFALLE WITH CARDAMOM

Vanilla flavoured caster sugar is easily prepared. Simply place 1-2 vanilla beans in a screw-top jar, fill with caster sugar and leave for 2 weeks. Keep topping up the sugar after use; then it can be used for months.

- 600 ml/1 pt semi-skimmed milk
- 1 medium egg
- 50 g/2 oz vanilla flavoured caster sugar
- 6 cardamom pods, split
- 225 g/8 oz fresh farfalle, dried
- 2 tbsp butter

Preheat the oven to 170°C/325°F/Gas mark 3 and lightly butter an ovenproof dish. Warm the milk. Beat the egg with the vanilla flavoured caster sugar, then gradually beat in the warmed milk. Add the cardamom pods.

Place the farfalle in the buttered ovenproof dish and pour over the milk mixture. Dot with small pieces of butter. Bake in the oven for about 45 minutes or until the pasta is cooked, stirring occasionally. Serve warm.

NUTRITION FACTS

Serves 4
Amount per serving 240g
Calories 348kcal/1468kJ

Total protein	13.1g
Total carbohydrate	49.6g
Sugars	21g
Total fat	12.4g
Saturated fat	5.6g
Polyunsaturated fat	1g
Monounsaturated fat	4.6g
Dietary fibre	1.2g
Sodium	222mg
Cholesterol	170mg

ORANGE ANGEL HAIR WITH FRUITS

If preferred you can use an unflavoured pasta for this dish; alternatively, try using a chocolate pasta. When making flavoured pastas, it is an excellent idea to make double the quantity and store half for later use.

NUTRITION FACTS

Serves 4
Amount per serving 96g
Calories 305kcal/1279kJ

Total protein	4.5g
Total carbohydrate	50.9g
Sugars	31.3g
Total fat	10.1g
Saturated fat	5.9g
Polyunsaturated fat	0.5g
Monounsaturated fat	2.8g
Dietary fibre	1g
Sodium	145mg
Cholesterol	82mg

- 100 g/4 oz orange angel hair pasta
- 1 medium egg
- 2 tbsp clear honey, or to taste
- ½ tsp ground cinnamon
- 40 g/1½ oz butter, melted
- 50 g/2 oz raisins
- 50 g/2 oz glacé cherries, chopped
- 50 g/2 oz angelica or other candied fruits, chopped
- 1-2 tsp icing sugar, sifted

Preheat the oven to 200°C/400°F/Gas mark 6 and lightly butter an ovenproof dish. Cook the angel hair pasta in plenty of boiling water for 1 minute or until "al dente". Drain, rinse under hot water and thoroughly drain.

Beat the egg with the honey and cinnamon. Stir in the drained pasta and melted butter. Mix the raisins, cherries and angelica together.

Spoon half the pasta mixture into the base of the buttered dish and cover with the raisin mixture. Top with the remaining pasta mixture. Bake in the oven for 25 minutes. Serve warm sprinkled with icing sugar.

COCONUT SPAGHETTINI

This recipe is based on a traditional Indian dessert, normally served at the end of the Ramadan fast. It is delicately flavoured with rose water and cardamom.

NUTRITION FACTS

Serves 4
Amount per serving 238g
Calories 434kcal/1813kJ

Total protein	10.7g
Total carbohydrate	36g
Sugars	22.5g
Total fat	28.6g
Saturated fat	19.5g
Polyunsaturated fat	1.7g
Monounsaturated fat	5.7g
Dietary fibre	5.2g
Sodium	99mg
Cholesterol	27mg

- 600 ml/1 pt milk
- 2 green cardamom pods, split
- 1 tbsp rose water
- 75 g/3 oz fresh spaghettini
- 4 tbsp clear honey
- 100 g/4 oz desiccated coconut
- 25 g/1 oz flaked almonds
- 50 g/2 oz ready-to-eat dried apricots, finely chopped
- 2–3 tbsp double cream

Place the milk and cardamom pods in a pan and bring to the boil. Reduce the heat and simmer very gently for 10 minutes; stir occasionally. Take care that the mixture does not burn.

Add the rose water and spaghettini to the milk and stir for a few minutes. Simmer for about 8 minutes, then add the honey. Increase the heat and boil for 2 minutes, then again reduce the heat to a simmer.

Stir in the coconut, almonds and apricots, and continue to simmer for 20 minutes, stirring occasionally until the mixture is thick and creamy. Discard the cardamom pods, stir in cream, heat for 1 minute and serve warm.

Orange Angel Hair with Fruits

Spaghettini

Tagliatelle

Papp

Garganelli